RISK
MANAGEMENT
FOR
ISLAMIC
BANKS

Edinburgh Guides to Islamic Finance
Series Editor: Rodney Wilson

Product Development in Islamic Banks
Habib Ahmed

Sharia'h *Compliant Private Equity and Islamic Venture Capital*
Fara Madeha Ahmad Farid

Sharia'h *Governance in Islamic Banks*
Zulkifli Hasan

Islamic Financial Services in the United Kingdom
Elaine Housby

Risk Management for Islamic Banks
Rania Abdelfattah Salem

Islamic Asset Management
Natalie Schoon

Legal, Regulatory and Governance Issues in Islamic Finance
Rodney Wilson

Forthcoming

Islamic and Ethical Finance in the United Kingdom
Elaine Housby

Maqasid *Foundations of Market Economics*
Seif Ibrahim Tag el-Din

www.euppublishing.com/series/egif

RISK MANAGEMENT FOR ISLAMIC BANKS

Rania Abdelfattah Salem

EDINBURGH
University Press

To my beloved parents

© Rania Abdelfattah Salem, 2013

22 George Square, Edinburgh EH8 9LF
Edinburgh University Press Ltd
www.euppublishing.com

Typeset in Minion Pro by
Servis Filmsetting Ltd, Stockport, Cheshire, and
printed and bound in Great Britain by
CPI Group (UK) Ltd, Croydon CR0 4YY

A CIP record for this book is available from the British Library

ISBN 978 0 7486 7007 9 (hardback)
ISBN 978 0 7486 7008 6 (paperback)
ISBN 978 0 7486 7009 3 (webready PDF)
ISBN 978 0 7486 7011 6 (epub)
ISBN 978 0 7486 7010 9 (Amazon ebook)

CONTENTS

FIGURES

TABLES

ACKNOWLEDGEMENTS

In the name of *Allah*, whose Power and Blessings have been continuously wrapping me throughout my life. My true indebtedness goes to my Creator, who paved the way for my success, and who blessed me with a loving family, supportive and critical supervisors, helpful and knowledgeable academics, practitioners, friends and colleagues.

No words can express my deepest gratitude, love and respect to my adorable parents for their continual encouragement during my work. They have always been creating the drive and motive for me to finish this book and my research work. I will forever remain grateful for their truthful concern, support and tolerance that they lovingly surrounded me with throughout my life. I am also grateful to my beloved brothers, sisters-in-law, nieces and nephew for their true understanding and immense support.

My deepest gratitude is well directed to Professor Dr Rodney Wilson, who encouraged me to undertake this project and provided me with critical feedback throughout the work. I further want to express my gratitude to Professor Dr Christian Kalhoefer, who supervised my PhD, which resulted in my taking on this project. I would also like to thank Professor Dr Ralf Klischewski and Dr Mehmet Asutay for their valuable feedback, continuous support, and guidance. Specifically, I would like to express my greatest appreciation to Mr Abdulkabeer Elbatanoni, who spent extremely long hours extending his experience in the field of Islamic banking, which contributed immensely to this book. I am deeply indebted to his contribution and patience. Last, but not least, I deeply thank my friends and colleagues who provided me with academic and emotional support, especially Dr Noha El-Bassiouny, my lifetime friend.

CHAPTER 1
INTRODUCTION

With the Islamic banking industry capturing the attention of the global financial community, specifically after the recent sub-prime financial crisis and the on-going European debt crisis, there is a growing demand for developing a comprehensive and integrated risk management framework tailored to Islamic banks. While risk management in conventional banks has been rigorously discussed in the literature by tackling its different aspects, risk management in Islamic banks remains an infant research area. Ariffin *et al.* (2009: 154) clarify that 'given the freedom of contracts and the understanding of *Gharar*, Islamic principles fully recognize risk that is generated by financial and commercial factors and elements extrinsic to the formation of the business transaction'. Consequently, risk management is critical to the development and sustainability of Islamic banking in order to enable them to comply with international regulations and stay competitive in the global financial market. Owing to its importance, this book aims at introducing an integrated framework for managing risks in Islamic banks.

The Islamic finance industry represents around 1 per cent of the world's global assets and has been growing by more than 20 per cent per annum since 2000 (IFSB 2010). More recently, the Islamic Financial Services Board (IFSB), Islamic Development Bank (IDB) and Islamic Research and

Training Institute (IRTI) reported that Islamic banking assets had reached USD 660 billion by the end of 2007 (IFSB 2010). Currently, the global market for *Shari'ah*-compliant assets is now worth USD 1.2 trillion. The driving demand, on both the corporate and individual levels, for Islamic financial services is among the factors that stimulate the growing sector (Hasan and Dridi 2010). The Islamic banking industry is a main contributor to the Islamic finance industry and represents a small but growing segment of the global banking industry. The vast growth of the Islamic banking industry extended to capture the eyes of large conventional banks to provide Islamic products through what is referred to as 'Islamic Windows'. As Islamic banks grow and operate in a global financial environment, they are faced by the challenge of maintaining competitiveness in the market. To stay competitive Islamic banks should provide competitive banking services and meet international banking standards, of which risk management is an integral part that ensures financial stability. In addition, Islamic banks should comply with the guidelines provided by *Shari'ah*.

It is acknowledged that banking business revolves around risk, where banks tend to make profit by offering services that transform risks (Marrison 2002: 1; Heffernan 2005: 101). Accordingly, the importance of risk management in banks is emphasised in theory as well as in practice through the Bank for International Settlements (BIS).[1] The BIS has issued various publications addressing the importance of risk management practices in banks, as well as determining the regulatory guidelines (Basel I, II and III). These guidelines aim at regulating banks, monitoring risk management procedures, and promoting a stable financial environment worldwide. As the financial industry becomes more interconnected and globalised, the impact of financial disturbances becomes contagious. This is witnessed through the recent sub-prime financial crisis during which the ineffective management of risks was among the causes of the crisis, which invites research into that area. Thus, there is a ripe area for research that aims at continuous improvement of the theory and practice of risk management, as any deficiencies in managing risks cause distortions to the global economy and financial industry.

Consequently, taking into consideration the growth of Islamic banks in a globalised and integrated financial system, and the importance of risk management, it is a necessity to construct a well-established and integrated risk management system for Islamic banks. The importance of risk management in Islamic banks is also recognised in practice through the work of the Islamic Financial Services Board. The IFSB is among the supervisory organisations designed to lead the industry towards a standardised regulatory framework and a transparent industry. It cooperates with the BIS on setting risk management frameworks and capital adequacy requirements for Islamic financial institutions, heading towards a strong regulatory framework that complies with *Shari'ah*. The framework provided by the IFSB aims at assuring the sustainability of the Islamic financial system within the international context. However, Islamic financial institutions currently face the challenge of understanding the inherent risks and designing an efficient risk management framework (Akkizidis and Khandelwal 2007). Islamic banks clearly lack a standardised identification of the risks underlying Islamic financial contracts, such as in the case of *murabaha* where market risk is commonly misidentified. Additionally, designing a risk management framework for Islamic banks is highly challenged by the lack of standardisation in financial reporting, the lack of applicable quantitative measures and the inadequate risk monitoring systems.

The paradigm of the Islamic bank business model is based on a set of principles that arise from *Shari'ah*. The principles of *Shari'ah* instil some changes to the nature of risks in Islamic banks. For instance, having the financing facilities backed up by a physical asset give rise to ownership risk and thus increases operational risk by embedding a new risk element that did not exist in the conventional banking business. Adding to that, *Shari'ah* principles cause some conventional measurement models, such as gap analysis, and mitigation tools, such as the use of some derivative instruments, to be inapplicable to Islamic banks. Hence, it is important to provide a comprehensive analysis of the risk management methods and tools that can be utilised in Islamic banks.

This research therefore aims at presenting an integrated risk management framework on the basis of existing risk management systems. The risk management framework presents a structured and comprehensive process for managing Islamic bank risks while operating in a global economy. This contributes to the development of the Islamic bank business model. Moreover, the book specifically bridges the existing risk management gap between conventional and Islamic banks.

The book is organised into eight chapters, including the introduction. Chapter 1 is the introduction that provides insights on the purpose of the book, the approach and content. Chapter 2 describes the risk management framework, elaborating on its applicability to Islamic banks. Within this book, the terms risk management framework and process are differentiated, where the risk management process refers to the steps underlying the risk management system, which are risk identification, assessment, mitigation and review. On the other hand, the term risk management framework implies a broader view of the risk management system in which both economic (*ex post* and *ex ante*) and regulatory analyses are illustrated. Thus, an integrated risk management framework captures the main risk management process, provides an economic analysis to evaluate and modify the risk management process, and ensures that regulatory aspects (such as identifying the different risk weights, required regulatory capital and capital adequacy ratio) are in line with the banks' operations. Taking it further, the chapter outlines an integrated risk management framework for Islamic banks that captures the risk management challenges faced by the industry.

Chapter 3 identifies the risks inherent in Islamic banks on two levels. On the overall level, the risk map for Islamic banks is presented with an analysis of the sources of each risk. Further, the specific risks that arise as a result of the nature of Islamic banks are also explained within the risk profile. Since Islamic banks hold different financing contracts on the balance sheet, identifying risks on the contract level is essential. Hence, the risk profile of each financial contract is identified by examining the individual contract elements disclosed by the relevant standard-setting authorities: the Accounting and Auditing Organization for Islamic Financial Institutions (AAOIFI) accounting and *Shari'ah* standards. Chapter 4 deals with the assessment of risks in which the widely practised risk measurement models are highlighted, followed by an overview of the current practices of Islamic banks with regard to risk measurement. Finally, a suggestion to improve risk measurement methods in Islamic banks is provided. It is mainly recommended that Islamic banks should develop a data set to enable the use of risk measurement methods; this could be easily achieved by adopting a risk coding system as suggested in this chapter. Chapter 5 describes the risk mitigation step, where mitigation methods are determined for each identified risk. In this chapter, mitigation methods are classified into methods for mitigating overall risks and contract risks. In addition, other suggested mitigation risks are highlighted, though not recommended, as such methods are still not fully accepted by all *Shari'ah* schools.

Chapter 6 then presents an application of the developed risk management framework for Islamic banks. Within this chapter, the presented Islamic bank model is developed and the risk management framework proposed to manage the risk management challenges of Islamic banks is elaborated. Moreover, some scenarios are used to exemplify the risk analysis process as well as the mitigation of risks. Chapter 7 highlights regulatory issues and provides some reflections on regulating risk in Islamic banks, especially with the implications of Basel III. Finally, Chapter 8 concludes with an analysis of the proposed approach for managing risks in Islamic banks and indicates the challenges ahead of an integrated application of risk management.

Note
1. 'The BIS, established on 17 May 1930, is the world's oldest international financial organization which fosters international monetary and financial cooperation and serves as a bank for central banks.' See http://www.bis.org/about/index.htm.

CHAPTER 2
INTEGRATED RISK MANAGEMENT FRAMEWORK

Not only do banks need to apply prudent risk management practices, but also an integrated risk management approach is essential to avoid crisis. In fact, risk management is a dynamic area, where its applications are re-visited in the aftermath of every crisis. Only recently, improvements to risk management practices and regulations have been suggested after the sub-prime crisis and amidst the European debt crisis. In any case, banks should and are asked to follow a comprehensive and integrated approach for managing risks. Islamic banks are not ruled out of this picture, especially when operating in a global financial system where, in some cases, Islamic banks follow conventional banking regulations. However, Islamic banks, being part of a relatively less-developed industry, face many challenges in implementing adequate risk management practices. Islamic banks may typically apply some conventional risk management practices, modify some applications to fit the specific nature of Islamic banks, or develop new approaches to manage the risks. While some challenges hold back Islamic banks from a comprehensive and integrated approach towards managing risks, the importance of such an approach should be recognised in view of recent financial crises. This chapter describes the risk management framework, elaborating on its applicability to Islamic banks, capturing the main steps of a risk management process. The chapter also explains the risk management challenges faced by Islamic banks and finally provides an integrated approach for managing risks in Islamic banks, which captures the risk management challenges faced by the industry.

2.1 Risk management framework

Banks are the backbone of any economy and thus governments tend to ensure the sustainability of banking business all over the world. One function of banks is to transform risks from individuals or deposit holders, who are risk averse, and employ the funds in risky projects. The intermediation role is enhanced by a bank's ability to accumulate information and eliminate information asymmetry. During the past decades, banking business has become more active and has exceeded the traditional intermediary role, where banks engage in global investment activities, such as investing in the derivatives market and actively engaging in securitisation activities. Widening banking activities on the international level not only increases profits, but also exposes banks to a larger variety of risks. One clear example is systemic risk, caused by market disruptions, in which one bank failure leads to the collapse of the banking system.

As banking business revolves around risk, the importance of managing risks in banks has been emphasised for decades. Such an emphasis appears after every financial crisis when further risk management developments are introduced. One recent example is the suggested enhancements introduced to liquidity risk management through Basel III after the sub-prime financial crisis, which impose clear improvements to the quality and quantity of liquidity risk measures. Being the backbone of economies, banks seek to implement prudent policies and procedures and apply an integrated process to adequately manage risks. In general banks follow the same risk management processes, which would vary only slightly from one bank to another.

The terms risk management process, system and framework are used interchangeably, where the definitions, although providing the same risk management function, vary in their degree of comprehension. Risk management is a process that starts by identifying risks, going through having consistent and understandable measures for each risk, then choosing among the risk mitigation strategies. Finally, the process should conclude by establishing appropriate procedures to monitor the results, which is a very important step in any risk management process as it allows for constructive analysis. Added to the described steps of managing risks, an integrated framework and a day-to-day risk communication throughout the different operating levels are the foundation for a best-practice risk management process. Moreover, an evaluation of the resulting risk profile should be conducted *ex post* and *ex ante*. In this sense, we can differentiate between the terms risk management framework and process. Risk management process refers to the steps underlying any risk management system, which are risk identification, assessment and mitigation. On the other hand, the term risk management framework implies a broader view of the risk management system in which both economic (*ex post* and *ex ante*) and regulatory analyses are engaged. The risk management process is applied for each phase of analysis, economic and regulatory, within the framework (Pyle 1997: 2; Crouhy *et al.* 2001).

There is no 'single best way' for implementing an effective risk management process or framework since banks are not all equal. Yet, a risk management framework can be flexibly designed and adapted to match different banks' operations. In principle, adequate risk infrastructure should be established to support management policies. This adequate infrastructure requires qualified personnel, accurate data and integration of risk management operations with available technology. Accurate risk data should be ensured in order to allow for the use of the appropriate risk measurement methodologies that would best apply to each risk exposure. The emergence of models and risk management tools for quantifying and monitoring risks alleviates risk control decisions and enhances an efficient risk management process (Heffernan 2005).

There is no concise agreement about what constitutes an optimum risk management system; however, it is agreed that banks should follow an integrated risk management framework to achieve the desired practices of risk management. An integrated process allows management to monitor risk-return profiles at all operational levels and define corrective or enhancing actions. The description of the adequate framework, process or system varies from one bank to another, yet all descriptions are sketched around the importance of implementing a well-defined analysis and control process of risks, whether that is to be applied at the corporate level or the business unit level. An integrated risk management framework can be described as a system that applies the four main steps of the risk management process – risk identification, measurement, mitigation and review – through two phases of analysis, namely economic and regulatory analyses. The economic analysis is further subdivided into *ex ante* and *ex post*, as demonstrated in Figure 2.1 below.

A risk management process is often presented through four steps, as illustrated in Figure 2.1. The first two steps – identification and assessment – are referred to as the risk analysis step, which requires adequate analysis of risks faced by the bank. This is conducted through a thorough identification of risks followed by risk measurement/quantification.

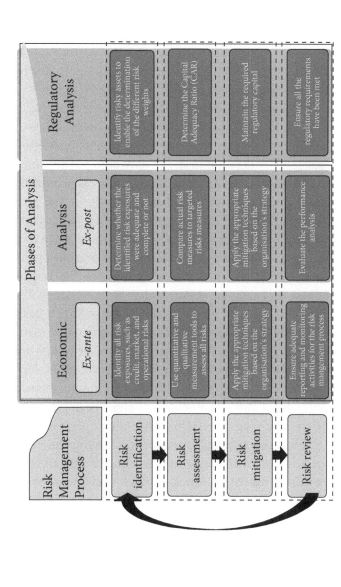

Figure 2.1 *Risk management framework*

Risk analysis is considered the backbone of the risk management process since it facilitates the decision-making process when determining the appropriate strategies to be used for mitigating the analysed risks. During the risk mitigation phase, senior management sets strategies to control the analysed risks according to their viewed importance. Finally, an efficient monitoring system is implemented in order to provide feedback and help in modifying future risk management procedures. This last step requires a critical review of the whole process after risks have been identified, assessed and suggested mitigation strategies have been put forward.

Added to that, a risk management process should be applied throughout different phases of analysis. The process is employed within the economic analysis phase, which includes *ex ante* and *ex post* phases of analysis, as well as the regulatory analysis. The economic analysis starts during the planning period (*ex ante*) and continues with the evaluation phase (*ex post*). The *ex ante* and *ex post* analyses enable managers to evaluate performance on a risk-return basis and compare actual performance with targets set by management. During the *ex post* analysis, previous results are assessed, while the potential future performance developments are analysed and accounted for during the *ex ante* analysis. The *ex ante* phase of analysis gives the opportunity to analyse risk-taking decisions, while the *ex post* perspective enables management to monitor risks. Taking these two perspectives when analysing risks is essential with all risk-management-related decisions in which analyses are to be conducted during risk events and afterwards. This paves the way for a better future decision-making process (Heffernan 2005). Furthermore, a bank's management ensures compliance with regulatory and supervisory issues that aim at maintaining a sustainable economic environment within the regulatory analysis.

In conclusion, the four steps of the risk management process should be implemented during each phase of analysis (*ex ante* and *ex post*). After the risk exposures are adequately identified, the assessment suggested within the framework comprises both qualitative (such as policies) and quantitative (such as statistical measurement models) elements. It is recommended to use a quantification model, when applicable, that is able to consistently capture different banking risks and that can be easily adjusted based on the complexity of the business. In this regard, Value at Risk (VaR) and Risk Adjusted Return on Capital (RAROC) are commonly agreed upon risk measures that qualify for such a purpose and are increasingly being accepted as the widely practised methods by industry regulators and practitioners (Crouhy *et al.* 2001).

Modern risk models introduce a bank-wide risk management concept where risk management is fragmented across different risks and business lines. For example, market risk analysis is based on quantitative methods and models, credit risk analysis is fundamentally based on qualitative techniques, while Asset Liability Management (ALM) requires specific risk measurement tools to define the appropriate funding and investment policy on the overall business level of the bank. Yet, the foundations of risk measures are comprehensive and allow risks to fit into a common basic framework by applying common concepts such as VaR (Bessis 2002: 64–6). According to Beder (1995), the BIS and the International Swaps and Derivatives Association, among others, declared VaR a fundamental risk measure for the best-practice risk management approaches. However, the level of sophistication of a bank's risk management programme should correspond to the overall level of risk and complexity of its business (BCBS 2009: 10).

The VaR model measures the economic capital (risk

capital) and is introduced by the Basel committee as a main component in risk management that provides a more flexible method to better assess and capture banking risks within the regulatory capital. However, the efficiency of economic capital as a risk measure is questionable since it does not always provide an early warning system for critical losses. That is especially clear in the case of financial innovations, where there is no appropriate historical data – on which risk models rely – provided in the case of new risks. Another reason is because interdependencies among risk categories are not fully captured. The recent sub-prime crisis provides a clear example with the case of Structured Investment Vehicles (SIVs) that were treated as low-risk off-balance-sheet items shifting to high-risk on-balance-sheet items and drawing away liquidity lines. Accordingly, intense scenario analysis and stress testing are used to assess areas of similar potential problems; these are important risk measurement methods because they reflect the possible risk effects on different capital definitions, such as economic and regulatory capital (KPMG 2008). Likewise, Scholes (2000) suggests that despite having the VaR as an accepted dynamic measure for determining the regulatory capital of banks, regulators should also elucidate the importance of applying other methods that help to plan for crises, such as stress testing, because the VaR analysis *per se* fails to qualify a bank as capable of meeting its obligations in time of crises.

Similar to VaR, the Risk Adjusted Return on Capital is another important measure for managing risks. RAROC has a two-fold function: it is used to allocate capital according to risks and for institution-wide risk management schemes (Ahmed 2006). RAROC allows an expanding line of business to reach an efficient allocation of capital based on the accompanied risks, thus managing risks relative to returns.

Moreover, using advanced applications of RAROC allows the bank to expand the base of products with a larger set of information through calculating the return generated from a certain transaction as compared to the required risk capital. Added to that, risk capital, also referred to as economic capital, has become a central concept of modern risk management, which is required to protect against large unexpected losses. However, its calculation represents a challenge based on the understanding of the underlying risks, which emphasises that the more risk is understood, the better is our ability to calculate risk capital. RAROC has become essential for integrated risk management since it allocates capital based on the associated risk, and thus enables the bank to determine different risk-return profiles. Finally, the last step within the framework, risk review, ensures adequate risk reporting and monitors risk performance on the business-unit level and the corporate level.

Once the bank has identified the proper risk analysis techniques the appropriate risk mitigation methods should be identified. Sometimes it is suggested that an appropriate process for the management of risks achieves the objectives of risk mitigation without putting in specific mitigation strategies. This directly leads to the final step in an integrated risk management system, in which a bank should insure an efficient reporting and review system throughout the different departments. Banks usually maintain solid accounting and disclosure standards that are then audited to meet the prudent regulation. On one hand, such a solid regulated system of financial reporting should be designed to assist banks in evaluating performance. On the other hand, banks should maintain and train sufficient risk management experts who are able to identify and evaluate the different risks faced by the bank. It is suggested that the risk-management function operate independently of the line-management units, where risk managers report directly to top management.

In general, in order to minimise losses banks should manage risks on the corporate level, business-unit level and transactional level (Marrison 2002: 7). At the business and transactional levels, risks are managed based on the type of risk and the amount of risk exposure. As for the corporate level, management tries to maximise the overall returns under a limited amount of risk by considering three core risk management decisions. First, is deciding on the desired bank's credit rating/creditworthiness measured by quantitative and qualitative measures set by independent agencies such as Standard & Poor's (S&P) and Moody's. Credit ratings are basically determined by the capital the bank holds against the risks taken, where the higher the capital-to-risk ratio, the higher the rating received, enabling a bank to access funds at lower costs. Consequently, the capital-to-risk ratio should be in line with the creditworthiness the bank targets. This leads to the second core decision of calculating the amount of available capital to decide whether an increase of the bank's capital is necessary. Such an increase could either be through issuing shares or retaining profits. Finally, a bank's management is able to calculate the total risk capacity, which equals the probability of default multiplied by the available capital. Hence, the bank's management decides on the amount of risk to be allocated to each business unit, such as corporate lending or trading. After allocating risk limits, the bank also determines a target required rate of return, referred to as the hurdle rate, in return for the given risk limits.

A successful application of the risk management framework can only be insured through developing an integrated reporting and monitoring system for the risk process. Reporting and monitoring of risks are ensured through the last step of the risk management process – risk review – where reporting and monitoring activities should flow from top-down and bottom-up operational levels. During the *ex ante* phase, the risk reporting and monitoring system is set and ensured throughout the different departments and levels of operations. Further, the designed reporting and monitoring systems are evaluated as part of the *ex post* phase. Also, a bank should be aware of the reporting requirements set by the relevant regulatory and supervisory authorities.

To sum up, the proposed framework provides an integrated and comprehensive risk management system that is equally applicable to conventional and Islamic banks. The framework captures the main risk management process, provides an *ex post* analysis to evaluate and modify the risk management process, and ensures that regulatory aspects are in line with the banks' operations.

2.2 Risk management challenges in Islamic banks

Islamic banking activities, although not completely varying from conventional banking, result in a special banking model. Managing risks in the Islamic banking model is not by any means an easy task. In practice, Islamic banks are faced with some challenges that hinder adequate management of risks. These challenges can be summarised in five main points. The first challenge is the inappropriate identification of Islamic banking risks caused by the intermingling and unique mixture of risks that result from the various activities conducted by Islamic banks. Second, Islamic banks need more rigorous risk assessment techniques that capture the uniqueness of the Islamic financial structure. Third, the lack of liquid assets as well as the non-existence of a lender of last resort, along with the minimal use of

Figure 2.2 *Risk management challenges faced by Islamic banks*

securitisation, increases liquidity risk among Islamic banks. Fourth, *Shariʿah*-compliant mitigation strategies are yet to be developed and maintained within financial markets; hence, this requires an adequate deployment of financial engineering techniques. Finally, Islamic banks lack an integrated risk management framework that outlines the existing challenges. Figure 2.2 summarises the risk management challenges faced by Islamic banks.

The first challenge, represented by the inadequate identification of risks, is mainly driven by the bundling of risks and the transformation of credit and market risks throughout different phases of an Islamic contract. Moreover, the unique structure of the Islamic banking model makes the identification process unconventional, and hence challenging. The mixture and structure of Islamic banks' risks vary more than that of conventional banks. The structure of the balance sheet of the Islamic banking model provides various financing (e.g. *murabaha* or *ijara*) and profit-loss-sharing (PLS, e.g. *musharaka* or *mudaraba*) instruments on the asset side. Each instrument holds different sources of risks based on its contractual agreement, for example, the sources of operational risks in an *ijara* contract will differ from the operational risks inherent in a *murabaha* contract. To adequately manage risks, Islamic banks should embrace a detailed analysis of the underlying risks.

Sundararajan (2007: 40–64) acknowledges that recognising the specific bundling of risks in individual Islamic financial contracts and the associated correlations are a major challenge, because all contracts include a mix of credit and operational risks. For instance, in the case of a *salam* contract, the bank is exposed to counterparty risk upon the advance payment, market risk for delivering the commodity as specified in the contract and operational risk for holding the physical asset. Moreover, each contract undergoes more than one stage, each involving a different mixture of risks. It is better for Islamic banks to assess risks for each contract/instrument separately to facilitate the risk management process, because the implications of the importance of each risk vary based on the nature of the contract/instrument (Ariffin *et al.* 2009). However, the individual assessment should be integrated at the overall bank level in a way that considers correlation among various risks. Yet, Islamic banks attempt to manage risks individually, rather than in an integrated manner, ignoring the fact that these risks are mixed and probably correlated (Akkizidis and Khandelwal 2007). Accordingly, an essential step towards maintaining a clear identification of risks is to un-bundle the mix of risks, elaborating on the sources of each risk arising as a result of each contractual agreement, and to determine their possible correlations. This can be done by understanding the main features upon which the contractual agreements are based, which are provided by the AAOIFI standards.

The assessment of risks represents the second challenge towards adequate risk management in Islamic banks. Currently, Islamic banks depend on qualitative methods to measure some risks, such as the use of credit scoring as a measure of credit risk. However, the use of quantitative risk measurement methods is essential to define the value of the identified risks and determine if further actions are required, such as applying a 'stop loss' scenario or minimising/increasing any of the financing activities. Such decisions are taken by the bank's management after analysing the returns relative to the underlying risks. Accordingly, the risk-return analysis is critical at this stage. Islamic banks lack sufficient data to conduct such analysis and it is even challenged that Islamic banks require more rigorous measurement techniques to capture the integrated risk structure. Hence, it is important that Islamic banks start by identifying the risk measurement models suitable for each set of risks, and accordingly monitor and report the risks. Such a process would eventually lead to developments in the utilised risk measurement methods. Among the challenges facing risk assessment for Islamic banks is the difficulty in deciding on the appropriate assessment approach, either qualitative or quantitative, for each type of risk. This can be solved by having a clear understanding of the nature of each identified risk, which will provide the ability to identify the appropriate assessment tool to be utilised. Other challenges, such as developing an Islamic benchmark or the high cost of allocating advanced risk models, also remain a point of argument among researchers. In any case, both quantitative and qualitative risk measures must be backed up by scenario analysis to strengthen the risk assessment. Scenario-based analysis, specifically stress testing, is critical to minimise the third risk-management challenge – liquidity management – which is caused by the lack of *Shari'ah*-compliant instruments. Such analysis helps in determining the liquidity position of the bank under different market conditions and, accordingly, it enables the bank to set mitigation strategies and be prepared for other different scenarios.

Liquidity management requires keeping liquid assets for a bank to meet its short-term obligations on time. When illiquidity problems arise, banks turn to interbank or central bank lending. Conventional banks manage their liquidity requirements through money-market products and interbank activities to avoid having idle cash in the bank. However, Islamic banks, in principle, have limited access to Islamic money-market products and prohibit interbank activities that involve interest. Hence, Islamic banks hold higher levels of liquidity, which negatively affects their profitability measures (Brown *et al.* 2007). Managing liquidity in Islamic banks represents a significant challenge for two reasons. First, Islamic banks lack liquid *Shari'ah*-compliant instruments, since *Shari'ah* law restricts assets securitisation that takes the form of debt instruments except when it is traded at par value. This specifically curtails diversification and restricts the banks' ability to manage maturity profiles of assets and liabilities. Second, it is difficult to access funds from existing capital markets as there is no interbank market for Islamic banks. Moreover, unlike conventional banks, the function of 'the lender of last resort' does not exist under Islamic banking operations because it is based on interest, which is prohibited (Archer and Abdel Karim 2007).

In their early stages, Islamic banks were stuck with high liquidity levels due to high growth of deposits versus loans and investment opportunities. In turn, Islamic banks relied heavily on conventional banks for employing their liquidity, which has often meant a lower return to Islamic investors as a result of a second layer of intermediation. However, due to the increased integration with international markets, Islamic banks are becoming more efficient in managing their own investments and channelling sources of funds to users of funds. Nevertheless, Islamic banks still rely on conventional banks when seeking financial engineering expertise since the former lacks the in-house expertise to develop *Shari'ah*-compliant products (Iqbal and Molyneux 2005). Currently, each Islamic bank uses its own strategy to hold a sufficient liquid portion of investment accounts that acts as a cushion against liquidity runs (Ariffin *et al.* 2009). This may have a negative impact on the bank's profitability if large amounts of idle cash are held from the invested amounts. In an attempt to solve this problem, the Bahraini monetary authorities have employed *Shari'ah* advisors to assist with auditing and developing short-term financial instruments, aiming to provide liquidity for Islamic financial markets and, hence, to solve one of the major challenges facing Islamic finance (Khan and Bhatti 2008).

Similar to the liquidity risk management challenge, risk mitigation is lagging behind for the Islamic finance industry. Islamic banks clearly lack sufficient and compatible *Shari'ah*-compliant mitigation strategies, which requires further research to design the appropriate *Shari'ah*-compliant techniques. Until more appropriate techniques are developed, an Islamic bank can select the most adequate techniques within those existing in the financial market. Finally, Islamic banks lack an integrated risk management framework that outlines the existing challenges. Despite the importance of having a comprehensive and integrated system for managing risks in Islamic banks to sustain industry growth, two main obstacles hinder that approach. First, is the cost of integrating, compiling and analysing information from different business lines/units and, second, is the regulatory cost imposed on the banking business, for example capital and liquidity requirements set by regulators (Cumming and Hirtle 2001). The next sections introduce an integrated risk management system in which risks can be easily reported, compiled and analysed.

2.3 Integrated risk management in Islamic banks

Among the lessons learnt from conventional banks' major risk events are that banks should maintain a full understanding of the business, ensure there are internal controls and monitoring systems within an integrated risk management process (Crouhy *et al.* 2001), as well as be aware of the complexity of the current financial markets that lead to the concentration of risks as a result of financial innovations and model risks (Das 2006). The conventional banking system has exhibited different crises ending with the sub-prime meltdown in 2008 and extending to the current European debt crisis. Believing that the Islamic banking industry is not immune to similar crises, experts in the industry should examine the causes of such events to learn their lessons. Ahmed (2009) suggests that the practices of Islamic finance could cause similar episodes within the Islamic financial sector, identifying three key factors of a crisis that could evolve in the Islamic financial sector: a deregulated environment, excessive risk taking and complex financial innovations. As such, a regulatory framework for Islamic financial institutions should be maintained in which excessive risk taking is strictly prevented and regulated. Moreover, developing complex (innovative) *Shari'ah*-compliant financial instruments should be minimised and controlled, particularly since the risks of Islamic financial instruments are not yet easily comprehendible. Risks within the Islamic financial industry should be managed through an integrated framework to control such events.

To attain a reasonable assessment of the underlying risks, a holistic perspective of the financial system must be realised (Greuning and Iqbal 2008). For Islamic banks to achieve an effective management of the underlying risks, a complete analysis and adequate understanding of the risks, regulatory system, market/s, and financial and economic environment under which the bank operates must be obtained. Accordingly, a risk management framework should be developed to analyse and manage the underlying risks of Islamic banks in a comprehensive manner. Moreover, when identifying risks, analysing the financial and economic environment should not be ignored, as they have a great impact on the level and density of risks. As this book does not focus on a specific economic or financial environment, but rather addresses universal Islamic banks with varying operating models, specific economic analysis will be ruled out despite its importance.

One important element that must be considered when designing an integrated risk management system for Islamic banks is to account for the risk management challenges faced by banks in the industry. In other words, whatever the system proposed to manage risks it should eventually propose a solution for each of the previously mentioned challenges. Hence, designing a framework as presented in Figure 2.1 would be the guiding path for Islamic banks to manage risks in an integrated manner, solving the listed challenges facing Islamic banks. The framework implements the risk management process through the economic analysis phase (*ex post* and *ex ante*) and the regulatory analysis phase. Adequate analysis and mitigation of risks is essential to enable banks to evaluate their performance relevant to their risk profiles. Accordingly, the framework aims at evaluating the performance of the bank on a risk-return basis while comparing it with pre-identified targets.

Regarding the first challenge, in which risk identification is not a clear process in Islamic banks, risks should be identified through the three phases of analysis: *ex post*, *ex ante* and regulatory analysis. Throughout the economic analysis (*ex post* and *ex ante*), the sources of risks are identified on the basis of the contractual agreements as well as on the overall business model. Risks based on the contractual level are determined by reviewing the elements of each contract underlying each financing instrument as stipulated by the AAOIFI standards. The overall sources of risks are identified based on the Islamic bank operational model, which appears similar to the conventional classification of overall bank risks. This helps the banking firm to ensure that all underlying risks are clearly taken into consideration before proceeding to the quantification process. Furthermore, it should be ensured that all risks inherent in every financing activity, as well as those that appear solely on the balance sheet, such as displaced commercial risk and withdrawal risk, are also included within the identified risks.

Once the first challenge is accounted for, it would be easy to choose among the widely practised assessment methods, either qualitative or quantitative, to measure the degree and severity of the risks. As the main aim of the framework is to conduct a risk-return analysis, measures that specifically address these elements should be used, such as the RAROC. Moreover, if risks are well identified, monitored and reported through the framework, Islamic banks will have the required data to move to the more sophisticated and advanced measurement methods. Nevertheless, building a suitable database would require a high level of cooperation among Islamic banks.

Having clearly analysed the risks, a bank will be able to decide on the efficiency of the selected mitigation tools, throughout the economic analysis. In addition, being able to identify the liquidity risk position of the bank, suitable liquidity management tools can then be easily decided upon by screening capital market opportunities. This approach of managing risks in an integrative manner, followed by the final step of reviewing the risk performance, will result in an improved process that leads to an effective management of risks. It ensures monitoring of the different activities through an effective reporting system and adequate flow of information within the bank (top-down and bottom-up flow of information). By following an integrated and comprehensive approach of managing risks, the fifth challenge of the lack of an integrated risk management system for Islamic banks would have been met.

Furthermore, the regulatory analysis is designed to ensure that a bank complies with the proposed regulatory framework of Islamic banks, both at the local and international levels. During this phase, risk analysis should result in identifying risk weights as stipulated by the underlying regulations, which specify the required regulatory capital that should be met by the bank. The importance of designing a regulatory framework is also recognised by Sundararajan and Errico (2002) as one important factor to be considered by effective risk management within Islamic banking systems. However, regulatory issues vary according to the system in which a bank operates. The IFSB (2005) guidelines represent the sole available risk management regulatory guidelines for Islamic financial institutions. It is worth noting that some governments have undertaken projects aimed at adapting Basel II to Islamic banks, such as the Kuwaiti government.[1] Yet, after the sub-prime crisis and the amendments imposed to Basel II, governments and supervisory authorities that aim at regulating Islamic banks should be aware of the implications of the Basel III accord upon their undertaken projects.

The remaining chapters elaborate on each of the steps in the risk management process and provide an application of the presented risk management framework to Islamic banks by the end of the book. However, it should be clarified that for an adequate application of the framework, the following points have to be noted. First, the framework must be within the main tenets of *Shari'ah*. This implies that '*Shari'ah* screening' should be embedded within the economic analysis phase throughout the whole process of risk management (i.e. analysis and mitigation). *Shari'ah* screening should be conducted by *Shari'ah* scholars, who will exclude any prohibited activities and any instruments that contradict the *Shari'ah* principles. Laldin and Mokhtar (2009) suggest that *Shari'ah* screening should be applied at two stages: before engaging in an investment and while deciding on how to manage the risk exposures. Hence, *Shari'ah* scholars ought to be involved in the process of risk management. Accordingly, it is recommended that *Shari'ah* screening is conducted through the involvement of two *Shari'ah* supervisory boards – external and internal – where the internal *Shari'ah* board is responsible for supervising existing and new financial products to ensure *Shari'ah* compliance and the external board supervises the approvals provided by the internal *Shari'ah* board (Ghoul 2008b). Currently, the process of *Shari'ah* screening varies among Islamic banks as there is a lack of a globally recognised screening framework and a lack of independent *Shari'ah* scholars/experts. Ghoul

(2008b) presents the screening process of Dubai Islamic Bank (DIB) as an example of an Islamic bank that applies the two stages of *Shari'ah* screening. They employ internal *Shari'ah* experts within the development phase of financial products and the developed products are then audited by an external *Shari'ah* committee.

Second, full disclosure of information to all stakeholders should be ensured by the bank, as transparency needs to be enhanced in financial reporting. Such disclosures are even more essential in an Islamic bank relative to its conventional counterpart, since deposit holders in an Islamic bank have higher incentives to monitor the bank's performance as their returns are highly dependent on the performance. Similarly, Sundararajan (2004) explains that disclosure of risk information, in addition to risk measurement, are key issues in implementing and enhancing a risk management strategy. Examples of essential information to be disclosed are the bank's operating strategy, profit distribution strategy and treatment of the Profit Equalisation Reserve (PER) and Investment Risk Reserve (IRR). It is worth noting that among an examined sample of the world's largest Islamic banks, Al-Baraka bank was the only Islamic bank that disclosed both PER and IRR, but with no reference to a specific profit distribution strategy.

The third important factor upon which the framework should be based is following unified accounting and reporting systems, as well as uniform *Shari'ah* standards. The AAOIFI proposes a uniform set of accounting and *Shari'ah* standards, which should be followed by Islamic banks. This will minimise operational risk by decreasing system and *Shari'ah* risks. According to Nedal (AAOIFI 2008a: vii), Secretary General of the AAOIFI, these standards have been implemented by Islamic banks operating in a number of countries, such as Bahrain, Sudan, Malaysia, Qatar, Saudi

Arabia, Dubai, Syria, Lebanon and Singapore. By following the AAOIFI accounting standards, disclosure of IRR and PER becomes a basic concept that should be implemented by Islamic banks. Such measures are considered corner stones in covering overall bank risks, as discussed later within the mitigation strategies.

As financial intermediaries, Islamic banks hold similar risks to their conventional counterparts. Yet, to have a clear understanding of Islamic banks' risk map, risks should be classified on different levels. Applying the first step of the risk management process, the next chapter elaborates on the identification process and classification of the various risks in Islamic banks.

Note

1. Based on an interview conducted with Abdulkabir Elbatanoni (2010), Senior Consultant of Islamic Banking, currently with the Ahli United Bank, Kuwait.

CHAPTER 3
RISK IDENTIFICATION

Islamic banks witness a similar risk map as their conventional counterparts where risks are mainly categorised into financial and operational risks. Financial risks are classified into credit, market and liquidity risks, as well as equity risks in the case of Islamic banks. Operational risks are divided into internal operational and external operational (business) risks. Even though the main risk categories are common in the banking industry, the sub-categories of risks in Islamic banks vary, such as in the case of market and operational risks. In general, the risk map of Islamic banks appears more complicated, with risks varying from one contract to another. Moreover, some specific structural operations in Islamic banks give rise to risks that have not been emphasised before in the banking industry, such as displaced commercial risk. For these reasons, Islamic bank risks should be identified on two levels. The first level identifies risks on the overall bank level where the sources of each risk are analysed. Specific risks that arise as a result of the different Islamic operational model, including *Shari'ah* risk, should be discussed in detail, elaborating on the sources of each. The second identification level deals with risks in each of the main Islamic financial contracts, since the sources of risk vary from one contract to another. For instance, market risk in a *salam* contract arises from price fluctuations of the goods/commodities to be sold after delivery, which is referred to as commodity risk. On the other hand, in an *ijara* contract, the sources of market risk can either be price fluctuations of the leased asset (commodity/asset price risk), change of the residual value of the leased asset (residual value risk) or, in the case of long term-fixed rental payments, fluctuations in the mark-up upon which the rental payments are determined (mark-up risk). In this way, the risk profile of each financial contract is identified by examining the individual contract elements disclosed by the relevant standard-setting authorities (i.e. the AAOIFI accounting and *Shari'ah* standards).

3.1 Overall bank risks

Islamic and conventional banks have similar functions while having both similarities and variations in their operational aspects. Both banking systems are financial intermediaries mediating between deficit and surplus units in the economy. Hence, it would be expected that some Islamic banking risks will resemble those encountered by conventional banks, such as credit, market and operational risks. Some suggest that, despite the similarities, such risks have different origins, impacts and implications in Islamic banks (Akkizidiz and Khandelwal 2007). Accordingly, Islamic bank risks, similar to conventional banks, may differ either in terms of their structure or severity. Other risks unique to Islamic banks stem from the distinct features underlying the operating model. For example, providing a home-financing facility through an Islamic bank will expose the bank to two additional risks than a conventional bank providing the same facility, namely, equity risk resulting from the asset ownership and *Shari'ah* risk (Haron and Hock 2007: 94–120). Furthermore, the practised deviation of Islamic banks from theory increases *Shari'ah* risk. Added to that, the challenges faced by Islamic banks when operating in a *Shari'ah*-compliant manner within a globalised financial system also increase risks to Islamic banks. One example is that holding a relatively larger amount of short-term assets, as an attempt to respond to the liquidity risk and the lack of *Shari'ah*-compliant liquid assets, increases Islamic banks' risks on the institutional and systemic levels.

The classification of Islamic banking risks is tackled throughout the literature, where some scholars provide a classification of the different risks inherent in Islamic banks. In contrast, others focus only on those risks unique to Islamic banks. The way scholars map out risks varies from one to another. For instance, Khan and Ahmed (2001: 54, 55) categorise Islamic banking risks into credit, benchmark, liquidity, operational, legal, withdrawal, fiduciary and displaced commercial risks. Akkizidis and Khandelwal (2008: 36–40) group risks in Islamic banks into credit, market, equity, liquidity, rate-of-return, operational and legal risks. Moreover, Iqbal and Mirakhor (2007: 241, 242) discuss Asset Liability Management (ALM) risk, which results from mismatching the maturities of assets and liabilities on the balance sheet, as one component of Islamic banks' risk categories. On the other hand, some research limits the classification of risks to those that arise specifically in Islamic banks: commodity risk, rate-of-return risk, mark-up/benchmark risk, legal and *Shari'ah* compliance risk and equity position risk. Iqbal and Mirakhor (2007: 227–50) provide a broader view of risks faced by Islamic banks by presenting financial risks, business risks, treasury risks and governance risks as the four main categories of risks. Regardless of the classification method used to identify Islamic bank risks it is a fact that the risk profile of Islamic banks does not typically resemble that of conventional banks. Islamic banks hold unique risks, such as *Shari'ah* risk, commodity price risk, mark-up risk, rate-of-return risk and equity position risk, as a result of their operational variations.

The risk profile of Islamic banks exhibits a more complex and larger variety of risks than that of conventional banks. To analyse the degree of complexity and variation of Islamic banking risks, a classification of the risk profile of Islamic banks is presented as depicted in Figure 3.1. This mapping of risks resembles the risk map existing for conventional bank risks and helps to provide a solid understanding of the underlying risks and to spot the areas where risks vary from conventional banks. This approach, accordingly, enhances effective application of risk management in Islamic banks.

Bank risks are mainly classified into financial and operational risks, where financial risks are divided into credit, market and liquidity risks. However, an added risk to an Islamic bank's financial risk profile is equity investment risk. Operational risks are categorised into those arising as a result of internal factors and external factors, the latter being referred to as business risks. Operational risks arising from internal sources include systems risk, people risk, physical capital risk and legal risk, while systemic risk and political risk are examples of operational risks arising as a result of external sources. As a result of the specific nature of Islamic banks, *Shari'ah* risk, Displaced Commercial Risk (DCR), withdrawal risk and rate-of-return risk all clearly arise in the Islamic bank model, *Shari'ah* risk being classified under internal operational risks.

Historically, credit risk has been thought of as the most significant risk in a bank, as it was the main reason for major banks' historical failures, and thus has become crucial to watch out for and quantify. Credit risk refers to the variability of servicing loans, which arises from either the unwillingness or inability of a borrower to meet the contracted

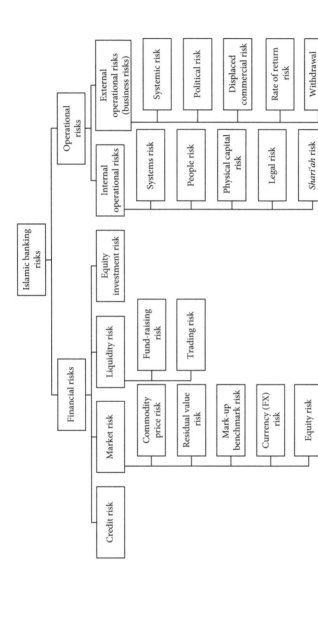

Figure 3.1 *Islamic bank risks overview*

obligations. If the payment of the cash flow of a certain loan is distorted as a result of an adverse change in the counterparty's ability to meet its contractual obligations, the present value of the loan/asset declines. Generally, credit risk increases with the increase of low-quality loans a bank holds on its balance sheet. The Basel Committee (BCBS 2000a: 22–6) summarises the main credit exposures as credit concentrations, credit processing and market/liquidity-sensitive credits. Credit concentrations result when the bank is exposed to potential losses that are relatively large when compared to the bank's capital. Banks should carry out thorough credit processing and assessment to minimise credit problems, even when such a thorough process is challenging, time consuming and requires a large set of information. Finally, market- and liquidity-sensitive credits impose more challenges to credit processes in a bank and thus increase credit exposure. Credit risk can also be classified into settlement risk, also referred to as Herstatt risk, and counterparty risk. The former arises as a result of failing to settle a transaction either by cash payments or asset delivery, the latter results from the non-performance of a trading partner that comes on the back of adverse price movements and is mainly associated with trading activities.

Parallel to conventional banks, credit risk is thought of as the most recognised risk in Islamic banks. Credit risk, given its traditional form, the non-performance of counterparty, is inherent in all Islamic finance modes to varying degrees. Specifically, it appears on the assets side of the Islamic bank's balance sheet, which is dominated by sale-based contracts (Sundararajan 2007: 40–64). Such a risk may arise as a result of internal or external sources, or moral hazard. When compared to conventional credit risk, Islamic credit risk appears to be higher for three main reasons. First, is the increased asymmetric information embedded in PLS contracts, where the obligor might not provide the appropriate information to the bank (financier) regarding actual profits that should be shared, which give rise to a higher probability of default. Akkizidis and Khandelwal (2008: 12) add that Islamic banks should be aware of the risk caused by moral hazard, specifically inherent in PLS agreements, where Islamic banks might be left with weak projects or start-up/small firms driven by the loss-sharing principle. As such, credit risk associated with PLS contracts, namely *mudaraba* and *musharaka*, is higher than that associated with sale-based contracts. Conventional banks usually avoid engaging in such contracts.

The second reason is the restrictions imposed by *Shari'ah* principles regarding the use of collaterals and penalties, where loss compensations are only permissible in the case of a clearly identified moral hazard. It is said that credit risk inherent in Islamic banks is intermingled with other risks, such as market risk, which makes it more severe than that in conventional banks. Nevertheless, it should be clarified that in conventional banks too market risk associates other types of risks, which is referred to as the 'grey area' accompanying credit and market risks, identified by Marrison (2002). The 'grey area' appears when credit risk is caused by unfavourable market conditions, which implies that credit risk in this case arises as a result of market risk. On a different note, Siddiqui (2008) argues that whether Islamic banks have relatively less or more credit risk varies according to the relevant institutional arrangements in each country, as in the case of Malaysia where Islamic banks show lower credit risks as compared to conventional banks.

Market risk, defined as the loss resulting from adverse market value changes, is basically the same in both Islamic and conventional banks. Market risk, which can either be systematic or unsystematic, is normally caused by market fluctuations associated with traded instruments (Heffernan 2005). However, Santomero (1997) relates market risk completely to systematic value changes that can be hedged but not completely diversified, such as variations in interest rates and value of currencies. Interest rate risk, being one of the most important components of market risk, is defined as the risk of losing due to unfavourable movements of interest rates. Bessis (2002) argues that banks usually determine the riskiness of a certain product by measuring its sensitivity to changes in market interest rates. Similarly, being concerned with the total market value, banks also measure the sensitivity of the market value to fluctuations in market interest rates. In Islamic banks some factors that affect the market value changes are different. The components of market risks in Islamic banks are: mark-up or benchmark risk, commodity price risk, foreign exchange (FX) risk and equity risk, where the first two are specific to Islamic financial contracts, while the last two are identical to the FX risk and equity risk of conventional banks. The former risks, which are specifically relevant to Islamic banks' market risk, are elaborated in the following section.

The third financial risk is liquidity risk, which is referred to as the inability of liquidating assets to meet short-term obligations. There are two dimensions of liquidity risk: one that deals with the availability of liquid assets and the other that focuses on the ability to raise liquid funds at a reasonable cost. Liquidity risk is very dangerous since it may arise as an outcome of other risks whose effect on liquidity has not been calculated. The effect of other risks may be severe, causing the bank to experience a liquidity crunch that might end with bankruptcy in its extreme case. Moreover, some banks face major problems and enter into 'liquidity runs', where depositors withdraw their funds and borrowers avoid acquiring loans, which leads the bank to a liquidity dry and thus jeopardises its business (Bessis 2002). Liquidity runs decrease the financial market confidence in the banking system and may cause systemic risk. This was witnessed during the 2007–8 sub-prime crisis, in the liquidity run suffered by the Northern Rock bank in the UK. During the past few years, liquidity risk has become the most important risk in banks; this was recognised by the BIS, which revisited the Basel Accord regulations and introduced liquidity risk management through Basel III.

The sources of liquidity risk are the same for all types of banks and financial institutions, yet when compared to traditional banks, Islamic banks are said to witness higher liquidity risk for different reasons. First, Islamic banks lack liquid *Shari'ah*-compliant instruments, since *Shari'ah* law restricts assets securitisation that takes the form of debt instruments except when it is traded at par value. This specifically curtails diversification and restricts the banks' ability to manage maturity profiles of assets and liabilities. Second, it is difficult to access funds from existing capital markets as there is no interbank market for Islamic banks. Moreover, unlike conventional banks, the function of 'the lender of last resort' does not exist under Islamic banking operations because it is based on interest, which is prohibited (Ahmed and Khan 2007: 144–7; Archer and Abdel Karim 2007: 223–35; Makiyan 2008; Ariffin *et al.* 2009). Accordingly, liquidity risk management in Islamic banks represents a significant challenge. However, Ariffin *et al.* (2009) state that each Islamic bank uses its own strategy to hold a sufficient liquid portion of investment accounts that acts as a cushion against liquidity runs. This may, however, have a negative impact on the bank's profitability if large amounts of idle cash are held away from the invested amounts.

Operational risk is crucial in the banking industry and

is incorporated in all banking activities, and thus the Basel committee issued its second Basel Accord to account for operational risk in the regulatory requirements. Operational risk is defined by the Basel Committee on Banking Supervision (BCBS 2001: 27) as 'the risk of direct or indirect losses resulting from inadequate or failed internal processes, people, and systems, or from external events'. However, within this context operational risk is observed with a broader view, representing the second category of bank risks, where operational risks may arise as a result of either internal or external factors. Sources of internal operational risks are physical capital risk, people risk (internal/external fraud), legal risk, systems risk and *Shari'ah* risk; except for the latter risk, these are identified by the BIS as the four main causes of (internal) operational risk. *Shari'ah* risk is explained in the next section.

Physical capital is dominated by technological/system failures; however, banks usually hedge towards the possible damage of some physical assets by insurance against risks such as fire. People or human capital risk arises as a result of human errors, such as poor settlement of different transactions/commitments, failure in processing information and inadequate record keeping, reporting and monitoring. In addition, lack of compliance with the bank's policies, as well as internal and external fraud, are also typical examples of operational risk caused by people/human capital, the latter being considered among the most dangerous risks a bank might face. Legal risk arises from different business practices and is defined by Santomero (1997: 10) as the risk that appears either directly or indirectly embedded in financial contracts that usually stems from management and employees' activities. Any of the above-mentioned events can result in unfavourable consequences that greatly affect banks' profits. The EUR 4.9 billion loss incurred by Société

Générale in early 2008 is one clear example of operational risk. This loss came as a result of an individual trader who extensively jeopardised the bank's trading position (James and Andrew 2008).

Moreover, model risk is identified as being significant in a market that traditionally uses models to price financial products and measure risks, emphasising that extending modelling techniques to other risks, such as credit risk, will increase the importance of model risk. Model risk is defined by McNeil *et al.* (2005) as 'the risk that a financial institution incurs some losses because some of the assumptions underlying these models are not met in practice'. One of the major obstacles that hinder testing the reliability of models is the scarcity of data and inputs. As such, model risk can be considered as one component of operational risk resulting from the applied systems, in this case models. Similarly, the exhibited Islamic financial industry growth gives rise to challenges in developing appropriate systems tailored to Islamic banks. This results in an increase in operational risks, caused by possible flaws in allocating the adequate personnel and the appropriate informational systems. Also, some of the unique characteristics of Islamic banking contracts are associated with operational risks, such as potential misconduct in the case of *mudaraba*, as well as the appearance of ownership risk in cases such as *ijara* and *murabaha* where the bank has to own the asset/commodity before financing a certain customer, among others.

External operational risks are the business risks which an Islamic bank is exposed to that include macroeconomic concerns, political risks and systemic risks. External operational risks include systemic, political, displaced commercial, rate-of-return and withdrawal risks, where the last three risks are explained in the next chapter. Systemic and political risks to which Islamic banks are exposed are similar to those of conventional banks; nevertheless, systemic risk appears to be higher in the case of the Islamic banking industry, as a result of the absence of a standardised acceptable framework for Islamic finance contracts and disclosure practices. Additionally, the lack of transparency regarding financial information and *Shari'ah* rulings increases the exposure to systemic risk.

Moore (2007) suggests that Islamic banks, being more conservative by nature, have an advantage over conventional banks by not having the complex derivative products and trading activities which, historically, have given rise to the most catastrophic bank losses, considering the case of Barings and the recent sub-prime crisis as two significant examples. Moreover, excessive risky behaviour, which is among the most challenging sources of financial disturbances, is prohibited by virtue of *Shari'ah* rules, as it may be classified as one factor of *gharar* in Islamic finance, being a driver for contractual uncertainty. Hence, it is argued that Islamic banking operations might be less risky than their conventional counterparts. Added to that is the ability of Islamic banks, based on PLS contracts, to transfer risks to investment deposit holders who share in a banks' profits or losses, providing another layer of protection in addition to capital (Heiko and Cihak 2008). Nevertheless, this argument does not give consideration to the displaced commercial risk, among others, arising from having the PLS deposit structure on the balance sheet of an Islamic bank. This is discussed in more detail in later chapters of the book.

As such, it can be concluded that basically conventional and Islamic banks share similar mapping of risks with some variations that result from the differences underlying both banking models. Although the integration among risks has been emphasised for Islamic banks, the significance of this has also been recognised for conventional banks throughout the literature. However, the separation of trading and traditional banking activities in conventional banks cause such an integration to be commonly recognised throughout the trading activities where credit and market risks highly interact, such as in trading derivatives. In contrast, the traditional banking activities in Islamic banks represented in the main financing modes such as *murabaha* clearly incorporate an integration of risks. That is because Islamic banks use sale-based, lease-based, and equity-based financing, which entails not only credit (counterparty) and market (interest rate) risks, but also include other forms of risks depending on the selected financing mode. More elaboration in this regard is provided in later chapters. In all cases, whether conventional or Islamic banks, integrated risk management is a challenging job that requires prudent monitoring. The combination of the different financing agreements, which vary between profit-loss-sharing (PLS), sale-based and lease-based agreements, under a bank model, lead to an unconventional process of risk identification. This, in addition to the transformation of risks witnessed under the Islamic financial contracts, adds up to the challenge for Islamic banks.

3.2 Specific risks to Islamic banks

Risks that are said to be specific to Islamic banks arise mainly as a result of the different operational model entailed by the *Shari'ah* principles. Operational differences can be identified by examining the operational models of both conventional and Islamic banks, which result in a different mapping of risks. The main features that differentiate Islamic banking operations serve as the basis for identifying the changes to the risk profile of Islamic banks. As explained in the previous chapter, the structure of some risks, such as credit and liquidity risks, is standard for both banking systems, yet in some cases the severity of such risks might increase under Islamic banks as a result of operational differences.

Basically, seven elements outline the differences between Islamic and conventional banking operations, depicted in Figure 3.2. First, Islamic banks are based on *Shari'ah* principles, which give rise to *Shari'ah* risk that does not exist in conventional banks. Similarly, the prohibition of *riba* gives rise to rate-of-return risk and shifts the interest rate risk that exists in conventional banks to mark-up or benchmark risk in Islamic banks. Third, the fact that financing facilities, either PLS or sale-based, should be backed by a physical asset or a commodity, contributes in changing the structure of market risk by highlighting commodity price risk. Also triggered by the lending facilities that must be backed by an asset is ownership risk that arises as a result of holding or delivering the asset, consequently contributing to operational risk. In addition, PLS contracts give rise to equity investment risk and increase operational risk resulting from asymmetric information. Furthermore, the restrictions imposed on requesting collaterals and charging penalties expose Islamic banks to a higher credit risk. Likewise, Islamic banks are exposed to higher liquidity risk due to underdeveloped secondary markets and lack of interbank activities, which hinders the quality of liquidity management. Finally, displaced commercial risk arises as a result of the unique contractual structure of depositors (investment account holders) in Islamic banks, which is based on a *mudaraba* (PLS) contract. Each of the stated risks is explained below.

Classified under market risk, Islamic banks are subject to two risks that distinguish the Islamic bank risk map, namely mark-up and commodity price risks. Mark-up risk arises from market interest rate movements, which are used as

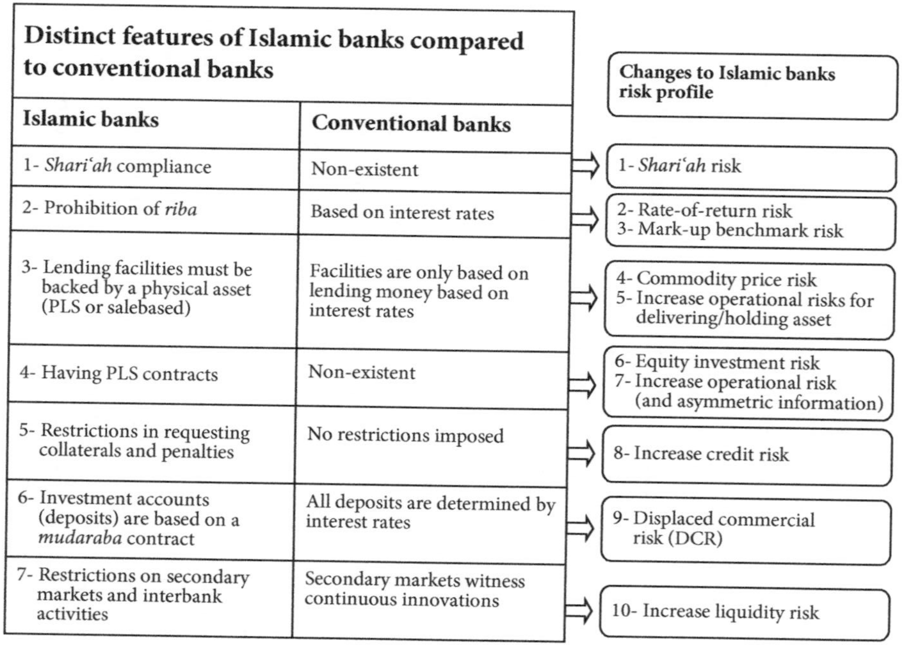

Distinct features of Islamic banks compared to conventional banks

Islamic banks	Conventional banks
1- *Shari'ah* compliance	Non-existent
2- Prohibition of *riba*	Based on interest rates
3- Lending facilities must be backed by a physical asset (PLS or salebased)	Facilities are only based on lending money based on interest rates
4- Having PLS contracts	Non-existent
5- Restrictions in requesting collaterals and penalties	No restrictions imposed
6- Investment accounts (deposits) are based on a *mudaraba* contract	All deposits are determined by interest rates
7- Restrictions on secondary markets and interbank activities	Secondary markets witness continuous innovations

Changes to Islamic banks risk profile

1- *Shari'ah* risk

2- Rate-of-return risk
3- Mark-up benchmark risk

4- Commodity price risk
5- Increase operational risks for delivering/holding asset

6- Equity investment risk
7- Increase operational risk (and asymmetric information)

8- Increase credit risk

9- Displaced commercial risk (DCR)

10- Increase liquidity risk

Figure 3.2 *Changes to the risk profile caused by the distinct features of Islamic banks*

a benchmark for pricing different instruments. Hence, the mark-up/benchmark, which is not subject to change upon signing a contract, is determined by adding a risk premium to that specified benchmark (Grais and Kulathunga 2007). As long as Islamic banks use conventional interest rates to determine the mark-up rates for some Islamic financial contracts, the mark-up risk is the same as interest rate risk. Furthermore, Islamic banks are exposed to commodity price risk – which should be differentiated from mark-up risk – as a result of holding commodities/physical assets to fulfil their contractual obligations. In *ijara* contracts, such as leasing equipment, both mark-up and commodity price risks are clearly distinguished: the asset (in this case equipment) is exposed to commodity price risk, whereas the fixed rentals are exposed to mark-up risk. In *salam* contracts, Islamic banks are exposed to commodity price risk during the period of the sale and delivery of the commodity (Iqbal and Mirakhor 2007). Additionally, in some contracts, such as the *ijara* contract, a residual value risk would be present, in which a bank faces the loss or a decline in the value of the leased asset. It is worth mentioning that commodity price risk in Islamic banks resembles what is known as performance risk in conventional banks, which appears when dealing in commodities that are transferred from one counterparty to another. Performance risk is transaction related and refers to a counterparty's performance regarding a specific transaction, where the transaction is backed by the value of the assets (Bessis 2002). On the other hand, performance risk holds other definitions: it is defined by Pyle (1997) as the losses incurred as a result of improper monitoring and includes model risk as one component that increases performance risk when inappropriate methods are used.

Another unique risk to Islamic banks is the equity

investment risk, which stems from exposures in equity investments (PLS instruments), namely *mudaraba* and *musharaka* contracts, on the asset side of the balance sheet (Grais and Kulathunga 2007). Equity investment risk is defined by the IFSB (2005a: 12) as 'the risk arising from entering into a partnership for the purpose of undertaking or participating in a particular financing or general business activity as described in the contract, and in which the provider of finance shares in the business risk'. As such, equity investment risk should not be mixed up with equity risk, where the latter is one type of market risk, while the former is a special type of Islamic banking risks that is concerned with capital impairments. Equity investments can lead to distortions in a bank's profits as a result of the high concentration of risks represented in credit, market and liquidity risks accompanying such instruments. Equity investments involve higher risk than other *Shari'ah*-compliant financial instruments because capital gain might be the only source of return; they may not generate a steady income and they do not have secondary markets, which imply a high early exit cost (Iqbal and Mirakhor 2007: 234, 235).

Shari'ah risk or *Shari'ah* non-compliance risk, defined as 'the risk that the terms agreed in a contract do not effectively comply with Islamic jurisprudence and thus are not valid under the Islamic law' (Sole 2007: 4), is another important component of operational risk that is unique to Islamic banking operations. Accordingly, different actions need to be explicitly considered for operational risk measurement (Sundararajan 2007). Rate-of-return risk, displaced commercial risk and withdrawal risk are all additional risks classified under operational risk. Rate-of-return risk is related to the rate of return provided to investment account holders (IAHs), also known as depositors in Islamic banks, who will be disappointed in the case of receiving returns lower than the prevailing market benchmark. It may be argued that rate-of-return risk is not specific to Islamic banks, since conventional banks are exposed to a similar risk known as business risk. However, conventional banks set a predetermined interest rate to deposit holders based on the market rates, and thus variations are of a minimal effect. To the contrary, Islamic banks distribute profits to their deposit holders based on the bank's profit and the depositors' share of investment; hence, the resulting rate of return may vary considerably from market rates. In practice, Islamic banks employ some mitigating actions to manage such a risk (see Chapter 5).

Displaced commercial risk is defined as 'the transfer of the risk associated with deposits to equity holders' (Ahmed and Khan 2007). It is classified under business risk, because it arises when an Islamic bank faces market pressures that lead to sacrificing part of their profit to depositors. This risk implies that shareholders may forgo part of their share in profits for the sake of depositors, to avoid depositors' withdrawals from a specific bank and movement to another offering a higher rate. Market pressures may result from other banks, either Islamic or conventional, providing higher returns. Similarly, withdrawal risk is caused by the variations of returns paid to deposit holders (IAHs) by business competitors (cf. Archer and Abdel Karim 2007). The rate of return on Islamic banks' deposits varies and is subject to re-pricing based on market rates, while on the other hand most assets have fixed returns and are not subject to price changes. Such a structure of the balance sheet creates a rate-of-return risk. It can be concluded that displaced commercial risk, withdrawal risk and rate-of-return risk appear to be interdependant, as will be clarified in Chapter 6. Adding to the above, the difficulty in enforcing Islamic contracts in a diverse legal environment, as well as the need to manage commodity inventories and monitor equity contracts, all serve as catalysts in increasing Islamic banks' exposures to operational risk.

Archer and Haron (2007) provide three categories of Islamic-specific operational risk. The first is presented by those risks specific to the execution of contracts, where the process is more complex and requires more steps than conventional financing. The second category relates to the risk of failing to comply with the *Shari'ah* principles and the bank's associated responsibility as a *mudarib*. Finally, the bank is subject to legal risks, which could either resemble those of other financial institutions or specifically relate to Islamic financing/investing contracts. Iqbal and Mirakhor (2007) add that people risk is another important aspect of operational risk that should be considered, providing the example of Dubai Islamic Bank, which lost USD 50 million in 1998 resulting from the non-compliance of an employee to the bank's credit terms. This caused the bank to face a 7 per cent decline in their deposits in only one day (Warde 2000).

To conclude, risks that are unique and arise specifically as a result of the Islamic banking model are benchmark/mark-up risk, commodity price risk, residual value risk, equity investment risk, *Shari'ah* risk, ownership risk, displaced commercial risk and rate-of-return risk. Commodity price risk, residual value risk and mark-up risk cause the market risk structure to vary from the conventional market risk structure. *Shari'ah* risk and ownership risk increase the risk sub-elements of internal operational risks, while displaced commercial and rate-of-return risks are risk components of external operational (business) risks. Other risks typically resemble those of conventional banks, such as foreign exchange risk, legal risk and political risk. Risks such as credit, liquidity, operational and business risks have the same sources as risks existing in conventional banks but show a higher severity within the Islamic banking model.

3.3 Risks in Islamic financial contracts

Islamic banks appear to be more complex as a result of the mix of financing tools replacing conventional loans. The complexity appears clearer when identifying the risks associated with each financing mode. This section elaborates on the sources of risks that arise on engaging in any of the Islamic financing instruments, by tackling each product on an individual level. Following the risk map provided for Islamic banks, risks are identified for each financing mode based on its contract's requirements disclosed by the AAOIFI accounting and *Shari'ah* standards (2008a, 2008b). Such standards are reviewed for each contract and the sources of risks are identified accordingly. Similarly, the accounting and *Shari'ah* standards also provide mitigation methods for each contractual agreement, which will be elaborated in Chapter 5.

On an individual level, the sources of risk that arise as a result of each financing contract are credit, market, operational and equity investment risks. As illustrated before, some market risks – FX and equity risks – are similar to those of conventional banks and hence are not tackled in this section. Instead, the main focus is on determining Islamic banks' specific risk factors that arise from each contractual agreement, where the market value of each contract is affected by a different set of risk factors (commodity price risk, mark-up risk and residual value risk) that depend on the pricing methodology utilised for each contract. Liquidity risk appears when any of these risks give rise to distortions in cash flows, thereby preventing the bank from meeting its financial obligations or adequately mobilising its financial resources. Hence, this section explores the sources of credit, market and operational risk, as well as equity investment risk when applicable, for each of the main financing contracts presented in the Islamic bank model: *murabaha*, *ijara*, *salam*, *istisna'a* and *mudaraba*.[1] Liquidity risk, among other risks, is illustrated within the overall risk structure of the bank in the following section.

Ijara and *murabaha* are favoured by Islamic banks as they are believed to have the lowest risk. Other forms of sale-based transactions, such as *istisna'a* and *salam*, as well as PLS-based instruments such as *mudaraba*, are less favoured by Islamic banks because they hold higher risks. Yet, the less-favoured financing facilities are also practised by Islamic banks to meet different customers' needs. In a *murabaha* transaction, a customer places a purchase order by requesting the bank to buy an asset/good on his behalf and promises to buy it back and pay in instalments. The main risk in such a contract lies in the fact that the bank must purchase the specified asset/good before concluding the *murabaha* contract, otherwise the transaction will not be *Shari'ah*-compliant, and the purchase order will not be binding. Thus, the bank faces the risk of buying an asset or commodity on behalf of the client who may refuse to fulfil his promise. Such a risk can be defined as a credit risk on the basis of not meeting an obligation (a promise in this case). The occurrence probability of credit risk in *murabaha* contracts is also increased by the restrictions imposed on penalties. An Islamic bank is neither allowed to impose penalties nor to charge additional payments to reschedule a debt in the case of delays in instalment payments.

Market risk mainly emerges as a price risk (mark-up risk), since in *murabaha* transactions the price is predetermined and is not subject to change upon signing the contractual agreement. Accordingly, the bank is subject to market fluctuations during the lifetime of the contract. Within this contract the bank is not subject to asset/commodity price fluctuations (risk) because the asset/commodity acts as collateral that is confiscated in case of defaults. Hence, the received amount (sale price) from the sale transaction after confiscation is an amount that mitigates credit risk, but does not affect the price of the contract.

On the other hand, operational risk mainly arises as a result of the bank's ownership of the asset/good during the lifetime of the contract, having to put up with any damage or destruction of the asset on delivery or after being delivered to the customer if it was proved that such damage was not caused by the customer. Archer and Haron (2007) add that under *murabaha* contracts, the bank is also exposed to the operational risk of the legal implications within the contract, such as not meeting the commercial objective of the transaction.

An *ijara* contract is defined by the AAOIFI (2008a: 264) as the 'ownership of the right to the benefit of using an asset in return for consideration', which clearly differs from a sale contract even when the lease period ends with the transfer of ownership. The *ijara* contract, for which the duration must be specified, is binding on both parties and cannot be terminated without the mutual consent of both parties. Nonetheless, the bank is exposed to credit risk caused by the risk of early termination of the contract in the case of *force majeure* or impairment of the leased asset that heavily affects its use. The terms of rental payments in an *ijara* contract are flexible, as the payments may be fulfilled throughout the duration of the contract or paid entirely in advance. Moreover, the rental payments (instalments) may be designed for fixed or variable amounts; however, in the case of the latter (variable/floating rentals) the amount of the first rental payment of the *ijara* contract must be clearly predetermined and the subsequent rental payments can be calculated based on a specified benchmark. Based on an agreement between the two parties, future rental payments may be amended as long as the lessee has not yet received any benefit from the leased asset for such periods. Yet, during the period of the *ijara* contract, if the customer delays any due payments the bank is not entitled to increase past amounts as they are considered debts (AAOIFI 2008b: 141–7), which give rise to credit risk within an *ijara* contract.

Similar to *murabaha*, the bank must own the asset before signing the *ijara* (lease) contract and is responsible for any defects of the leased asset throughout the duration of the lease period, which exposes the bank to operational risk. Impairments of leased assets might lead to credit risk, such as in the case of early termination. If the *ijara* agreement ends with a transfer of the ownership of the leased asset, referred to as *Ijara Muntahia Bittamleek*, this should be stipulated in a separate document (AAOIFI 2008b). Usually, the transfer of ownership occurs at the end of the lease period to avoid further risks.

With regard to market risk, there are three clear risk factors: mark-up risk, residual value risk in the case of *Ijara Muntahia Bittamleek*, and asset price risk in the case of operational *ijara*. *Ijara* contracts expose an Islamic bank to mark-up risk in the case of long-term fixed-rental payments. Residual value risk accompanies operating *ijara* contracts (leasing without transfer of ownership), where the bank faces the loss or a decline in the value of the leased asset (Haron and Hock 2007) since the asset is within the possession of the bank but being utilised by the customer. Finally, if sale is an element of the contract, as in the case of *Ijara Muntahia Bittamleek*, an asset/commodity price risk emerges because the sale price of the leased asset/commodity is predetermined and thus exposes the bank to market price fluctuations upon the transfer of ownership. In practice, operational *ijara* involves higher risk than *Ijara Muntahia Bittamleek* because, in the former, the ownership of the asset remains with the bank, which increases the bank's exposure to risk, while the latter form of *ijara* implies that the ownership risk of assets is associated with the client.

According to the AAOIFI (2008a), the *salam* is a type of sale that is defined as 'sale of a commodity for deferred delivery in exchange for immediate payment according to specified conditions'. Some elements of the *salam* contract must be satisfied to guarantee its legitimacy according to *Shari'ah*. First, the commodity (other than gold, silver or currency) for sale should be clearly identified to the contracting parties based on certain specifications. Moreover, the quantity, date and place of delivery should be known in a manner that eliminates uncertainty. Finally, the price of the *salam* contract must be paid upon concluding the contract. A *salam* contract is binding and thus is not subject to cancellation except upon mutual agreement, either a complete termination for full repayment of the amount paid in advance or a partial termination for a corresponding repayment. It is worth noting that the buyer of a *salam* contract is entitled to cancel the contract and recover the payment if the seller fails to provide the goods on the due date. In addition, similar to all sale transactions, a penalty clause in respect of delay is not permitted, based on *Shari'ah* rulings, and if the seller delays in delivering the goods due to insolvency, an extension of time for delivery should be granted free of charge (AAOIFI 2008b).

Therefore, credit risk, specifically settlement risk, in a *salam* contract arises from default or delay in delivering the subject matter of the contract. On the other hand, if the delivered commodity does not meet the required specifications, this exposes the bank to operational risk.

Furthermore, the bank is exposed to operational (ownership) risk throughout the process of delivering the goods, by being exposed, for instance, to unexpected storage costs, and is exposed to market (price) risk as a result of market price fluctuations of the goods/commodities to be sold after delivery. The method the bank utilises to determine the price of the *salam* should be taken into consideration when identifying the sources of market risk. For instance, if the bank bases the price of the *salam* relative to a market benchmark then the future fluctuations of this benchmark should be determined as the source of market risk, while if the price of the *salam* is simply based on the spot and future price of the commodity then the commodity price fluctuations should be identified as the source of market risk. For example, if the price of the *salam* contract is based on the LIBOR (London Interbank Offered Rate), then mark-up risk resulting from fluctuations in the LIBOR will be identified as the associated market risk factor. On the other hand, fluctuations in the commodity market prices will be identified as the market risk factor if the bank does not base the price of the contract on LIBOR, leaving the value of the contract to be determined by commodity market prices. This will lead to an appropriate assessment of the market risk of the *salam* contract.

It is common practice for Islamic banks to enter a parallel *salam* contract, where a third party acquires goods of similar specifications to those determined in the first *salam* contract. Such an engagement mitigates market (commodity price) risk on the bank's side since the third party should fulfil an immediate payment as stipulated by the contract. However, the parallel contract must be separate and independent of the original *salam* contract, as it is not allowed to link the obligations of both contracts (AAOIFI 2008b). Thus, the bank does not have the right to terminate or delay in performing its obligations for the parallel *salam* on the basis of any damage incurred through the original (first) *salam* contract. Accordingly, some risks within the parallel contract appear to be dependent on the degree of precision of the first contract. Such risks are attributable to credit risk on the bank's side. For example, if the seller of the original contract fails to provide the goods on time (credit risk) or with the required specifications (operational risk), the bank is consequently exposed to a credit risk of not meeting its obligations towards the parallel contract. In consequence, this may bring about operational risk, specifically legal risk and/or reputational risk. Moreover, the bank is exposed to operational (ownership) risk upon the process of delivery to the third party.

An *istisna'a* contract is similar to the *salam* contract and is viewed by some scholars as a special type of *salam* contract (AAOIFI 2008a). *Istisna'a* is defined as 'a sale contract of specified items to be manufactured or constructed, with an obligation on the part of the manufacturer or builder (contractor) to deliver them to the customer upon completion' (AAOIFI 2008b). Hence, the delivery of the asset or commodity in both *istisna'a* and *salam* are deferred to a future date. Consequently, the sources of credit, market and operational risks underlying a *salam* contract (explained above) typically apply to an *istisna'a* contract.

It is worth noting that identifying mark-up risk within product-deferred instruments (*istisna'a* and *salam*) will depend on the pricing method specified by the bank. If the bank bases the price of the contract on a certain benchmark, then the associated fluctuations will be identified as the market parameter, whereas if the bank does not use a certain benchmark in determining the price of the contracts then no mark-up risk is identified. On the other hand, commodity price risk is clearly identified as a market risk factor because the assets/commodities are not under the possession of the bank – not collaterals – and should be sold upon their future delivery for future, and hence uncertain, market prices. In this case, such contracts are subject to commodity price risk. Even when the bank enters a parallel contract to mitigate the commodity price risk, and agrees to sell the asset for a predetermined price, the bank is subject to commodity price risk through a possible increase in the market price of this asset upon execution, which is akin to the market risk involved in hedging through the spot and future markets.

Yet, the payment of an *istisna'a* contract is one main factor that is distinct between *salam* and *istisna'a*. In accordance with the AAOIFI (2008b), the price of an *istisna'a* contract may be paid in instalments based on the stages of delivery or completion of work (work in progress), where payments may vary accordingly but should not be calculated on a cost-plus basis. Moreover, while a *salam* contract is binding on both parties, the binding principle of an *istisna'a* contract appears to be controversial among *Shari'ah* scholars. The AAOIFI (2008b) stipulates that *istisna'a* contracts should be binding provided that the specifications of the type, quality, quantity and kind of subject matter to be produced, as well as the price and the time of delivery agreed upon, are not breached.

Similar to *salam* agreements, a parallel *istisna'a* is allowed in order to sell items, in the capacity of a supplier, with similar specifications to the first *istisna'a* contract, provided that the delivery date in the second contract does not precede that determined in the original *istisna'a* contract. Furthermore, contractual obligations for both contracts should remain independent (AAOIFI 2008b). In the parallel *istisna'a*, the bank is exposed to the same credit risk as with parallel *salam* contracts. In addition, the bank is also exposed to operational (ownership) risk during the parallel *istisna'a* upon receiving delivery from the contractor/ manufacturer, as per the agreement of the first contract, and prior to delivering the subject matter to the purchaser in the parallel contract (third party). It is worth noting that the manufacturer is liable for defects and/or maintenance costs and the purchaser has the right to refuse or accept delivery if the manufactured/constructed commodity/asset does not meet specifications. Nevertheless, it is permissible to include within the contract, upon the agreement of both parties, that the manufacturer/contractor is not liable for additional costs incurred as a result of unexpected or extraordinary market and/or economic conditions (AAOIFI 2008b). In this case, the bank, being the purchaser in the original *istisna'a* contract, is exposed to operational risk arising as a result of external factors.

Usually, an *istisna'a* contract is used to finance long-term construction or manufacturing projects. Such industries, by nature, constitute a high degree of operational risk as the result of their complex operative environment, where the sources of risks may vary per project, such as with the construction industry (Salem 2009: 17). Hence, based on the nature of the manufacturing and construction industries, Islamic banks are exposed to higher operational risks when financing activities through *istisna'a* contracts. Yet, despite the high operational risk, well-capitalised Islamic banks, such as Kuwait Finance House (KFH), Abu-Dhabi Islamic Bank (ADIB) and Qatar Islamic Bank (QIB), utilise *istisna'a* as a financing facility that ranges from 11 to 20 per cent of their total financing activities (the banks' 2008 annual reports). To the contrary, *salam* is not used as much in the Islamic banking industry.

Finally, it is acknowledged that Islamic banks deviate from PLS instruments because of the high risk involved in such contracts, regardless of them being the theoretical foundation of the Islamic banking model (Metwally 1997: 93; Hassan and Bashir 2000: 10–11). Since *mudaraba* and *musharaka* have very similar contractual agreements, for simplification the underlying risks will be elaborated through the *mudaraba* contract, which is recognised as being more risky. *Mudaraba* is a partnership agreement that may be conducted between the Islamic bank, as the provider of funds in the capacity of being *rabb al mal*, and agents or business owners, being the managing partners. Additionally, *mudaraba* is conducted between the Islamic banks' deposit holders, referred to as investment account holders (IAH), being fund providers and the Islamic bank in the capacity of the *mudarib*. The sources of risks discussed in this section are relevant to the former *mudaraba* contract, while the risks underlying the latter form are illustrated within the overall banking risks in the previous section.

The general principle of a *mudaraba* contract is that it is not binding and can undergo unilateral termination before the *mudarib* commences the business commitment. Furthermore, upon the execution of the contract, parties agree to set a specific duration for the *mudaraba* contract, which is considered binding till the end of the specified maturity and can be renewed upon the agreement of the parties. In addition, the *mudarib* (managing partner) is not liable for any losses except in case of misconduct or breach of the terms of the *mudaraba* contract (AAOIFI 2008b).

In a *mudaraba* contract the bank provides capital to a *mudarib* on the basis of sharing profits, while losses are to be borne by the capital provider only, with no obligation on the *mudarib*'s side unless losses arise from their proved misconduct or negligence. Accordingly, the bank, being the financing partner, is highly exposed to the risk of capital loss – equity investment risk (which is only relevant to PLS activities and is different from equity price risk) – in the case of incurred losses or termination or liquidation of the contract. In this case, the loss of the bank's financing capital is considered an equity investment risk rather than a credit risk, because in the liquidation of a *mudaraba* contract the bank has no liability over debtors as it is a form of partnership. Hence, unlike credit losses, it is not possible to claim any capital amounts before all other obligations of the *mudarib* are met. It is worth noting that according to the AAOIFI guidelines (2008b) liquidation of a *mudaraba* contract takes place due to any of the following: unilateral termination before commencement of the business activity; agreement of both parties; conclusion of the contract's maturity date; exhaustion of *mudaraba* funds as a result of incurred losses; death of the *mudarib*; or liquidation of the institution acting as a *mudarib*. Similar to other instruments, credit risk arises from any default or delay in profit or capital payments. Hence, the bank is exposed to credit risk in a *mudaraba* contract because the *mudarib* may not pay the amounts due to the bank on the basis of the agreed-upon profit share (AAOIFI 2008a).

The bank is not directly exposed to market risk through a *mudaraba* contract, since it may only appear within the operations of the financed project in which the bank is not directly involved. However, since the bank shares a percentage of the profit, then the returns provided to the bank depend highly on the profitability of the financed project, which is affected by market conditions. This may instead be classified under operational risk, since the profitability of the financed project depends on the quality of management decisions in assessing and selecting the profitable projects. Furthermore, the bank faces operational risk through its exposure to moral hazard, where the *mudarib* might provide misleading financial information or subject the provided funds to unusual risks, as the bank is not entitled to be involved in operational activities. Additionally, if the *mudarib* is not able to undertake the project, due to operational or market factors, that exposes the bank to operational risk as well.

In conclusion, on an individual contractual level, it is essential to maintain a clear understanding of the sources of risks associated with each financial contract. Such identification supports the bank management in assessing the overall risks to the bank and deciding on the appropriate control methods. It can be concluded that PLS instruments, represented by *mudaraba* within this context, pose the highest risk, followed by product-deferred instruments, namely *salam* and *istisna'a*. *Ijara* and *murabaha* are viewed to have the lowest risks. Ariffin *et al.* (2009) concluded with the same perceptions regarding the riskiness of the products through surveys conducted with regard to Islamic financing contracts. On the one hand, the perceived risk profile explains the limitations accepted by Islamic banks in holding *salam*, *istisna'a*, *mudaraba* and *musharaka* contracts on the assets side. On the other hand, it draws attention to the importance of considering the integration of risks.

While illustrating the various types of risks to which Islamic banks are exposed, the possible effects of integrating different banking risks, which is often the case, cannot be ignored. Such integration among risks is viewed as a driving force for possible financial crises, which might lead to systemic risks. Thus, it is vital to recognise the effect of incorporating different risks, especially when the integration is driven by mismanaging risks or ignoring their combined effect. Accordingly, many models were developed to quantify banking risks on an individual and portfolio basis.

The collapse of Barings bank in 1995 is an example of

how banks lose money from an event that involves several forms of risk. The bank collapsed as a result of a trader who made severe trading losses, hid them in fabricated accounts, and tried to recover the losses by trading with derivatives. The trader ended up reducing the bank's capital by USD 1 billion. The case of Barings bank included market, credit and operational risks, as well as an inefficient risk management process that could have avoided huge losses if risks had been discovered earlier (Marrison 2002). However, efficiently managing a bank's integrated risks is usually a challenging job that requires prudent monitoring. Das (2006) argues that real risks are driven by the complex structure of the existing financial markets backed by financial innovations and model risks. Financial innovations contribute to the concentration of risks, and thus increase the complexity of financial markets, by promoting the transfer of financial risks to the market through complex trading activities.

It is thus the role of the bank to adequately identify possible risks and their correlations. This step qualifies as the assessment process of the underlying risks. Yet, when determining the appropriate measurement tools, banks ought to consider the importance of integrating different risks with the same quantification method.

Note

1. *Musharaka* is not included within this analysis because it constitutes similar risks to *mudaraba*. *Mudaraba* was selected to be included within the conceptual model and analysis since, theoretically, it represents more risks than *musharaka*; hence, risk management applied to *mudaraba* can be easily adapted to *musharaka*.

CHAPTER 4
RISK ASSESSMENT

A very important step that is highly challenging in Islamic banks is the assessment of risks. The weakness of the risk assessment step breaks the chain of prudent risk management in Islamic banks. Hence, it is necessary to develop the approach to measuring risks in the industry. This chapter introduces the widely accepted risk assessment tools for each identified risk. Among these tools are Value at Risk (VaR), Expected Shortfall (ES), credit ratings, credit scoring, gap analysis, duration analysis and scenario analysis. Also, the chapter critically covers the current practices of Islamic banks in measuring risks and provides further suggestions on using more advanced measurement models, identifying the available assessment methods for each individual risk. The applicable measurement tools are identified to quantify each risk in Islamic banks, derived from the nature of each assessment method and the nature of each risk. For example, VaR, ES and scenario analysis can be used to measure all market risks except the residual value risk, which can only be measured using accounting methods. Duration analysis cannot be used to measure market risks except in the case of mark-up risk. Similarly, scenario analysis is an applicable tool to assess the different business (external-operational) risks, while rate-of-return risk (which is a sub-category of business risk) can also be measured by VaR, gap analysis and duration analysis, since the nature of this risk resembles that of market risks in conventional banks. Finally, it is concluded that developing a data set for Islamic banks' risks is essential in order to have a more advanced risk measurement system. Hence, a risk coding system for Islamic bank risks, which suggests that a certain code is given to each bank risk, is provided to facilitate risk reporting and monitoring. Applying a risk coding system will help develop a data base of risks in Islamic banks, which can then be used to measure risks and the correlation among the different risks.

4.1 Widely practised models

Risk measurement is the second step within the risk analysis process and is central to setting efficient risk control strategies, where banks should use consistent risk measurement techniques. Measuring risks enables banks to determine their risky capital and capital adequacy levels as well as being used by management to set limits for the maximum amount of risk allowed within different units/departments. Previous bank failures have shown that poor credit risk assessment is among the significant causes of banking problems (BCBS 2006b). This led the Bank for International Settlements (BIS) to focus on the importance of the assessment and valuation of credit risk, among other risks, and it provided guidelines to improve the quality of credit risk assessment and valuation of loans. The guidelines state that a bank should have a loan-loss methodology that includes:

- policies and procedures for the credit risk systems and controls
- detailed analysis of the entire loan portfolio

- a clear classification of the loans that should be individually evaluated for impairment and the loans that should be grouped into a portfolio with similar credit risk characteristics
- a proper process for an updated valuation of collaterals and other credit risk mitigants incorporated in the loan agreement
- the methods used to validate credit risk measurement and management tools, such as stress and back tests.

In addition, market risk is another important risk that is suggested by regulators and risk managers to act as an indicator of solvency risk. Thus, banks are urged to quantify market risk and provide plans for allocating scarce capital in case the risk takes place (Fallon 1996). After the sub-prime crisis and the more recent European debt crisis, liquidity risk has been stressed as a critical stimulus of crisis. An efficient allocation of capital is one important result of using adequate and valid risk measurement techniques. To determine the allocated capital, risk management units should determine the extent of risk specialisation for the identified risks, define the degree of centralising of the capital allocation process and, finally, set the methods used to evaluate risk adjusted performance. Basically, capital reserves are calculated for individual risks, and then risks are added up, while considering correlations among different risks, to determine the total capital requirement.

A proper risk analysis process requires apt identification of the possible risks and their expected probabilities. There are various types of risks identified and thus risk assessment tools differ depending on the type of risk addressed. Hence, some tools are used to quantify market risks but cannot be used for credit risk measurement. Moreover, the risk measurement method used in a bank is highly dependent on the management decision regarding the trade-off between the cost and time of using precise methods for measuring risks and the required measurement precision (Pyle 1997: 6).

Risks can either be measured on the overall banking level or for individual business units/products on a branch/ division level, where the usage of both external and internal risk assessment tools are recommended on the aggregate level. Credit ratings and supervisory risk assessments such as the Basel Accord and CAMELS (Capital adequacy-Asset quality-Management ability-Earnings level-Liquidity-Sensitivity to market risks)[1] are examples of external risk assessment tools (Khan and Ahmed 2001). The internal risk assessment tools are outlined below.

On a branch/division level different returns and risks are measured, but it is usually difficult to disaggregate multiple interrelated risks and their associated returns. It is acknowledged that integrating risks is more efficient for measurement purposes; however, risk quantification faces three main challenges when integrating different risks. The first challenge is that different risk types may follow different distributions. Next, it is not possible to apply the same time scale to all aggregated risks:[2] for instance, market risks are preferably measured on a short-term basis (e.g. one day), whereas credit and operational risks are calculated over a longer time period (minimum one year; Dimakos and Aas 2004). Finally, while it is important to measure the interdependence of risks, since all risks are to some extent correlated, it is difficult to measure such interdependence, which leads to the concentration of some risks. Such challenges impose a possible deficiency on the risk management quantification process. However, the mentioned difficulties vary among banks when assessing the risk adjusted performance depending on their business capacity and activity (Saita 1999; McNeil *et al.* 2005: 20).

Risk measurement methods have several approaches. Khan and Ahmed (2001) explain two approaches to quantify risk exposures. The first is the segmented approach, such as gap analysis used to measure interest rate exposures and Value at Risk (VaR). The second approach is the consolidated approach in which the overall risk level is assessed, such as the Return on Risk Adjusted Capital (RORAC). McNeil *et al.* (2005) provide a more detailed overview of the different approaches to risk quantification: the theoretical or notional-amount approach, the factor-sensitivity measures approach, loss-distribution measures approach and the scenario-based approach.

The theoretical approach is the oldest and simplest method for risk measurement and is defined as 'the sum of the theoretical values of the individual securities in a portfolio where each value may be weighted by a factor representing an assessment of the riskiness of the broad asset class to which the security belongs' (McNeil *et al.* 2005). This approach is commonly used with operational risk despite its major disadvantage of not reflecting the effects of diversification on the underlying risks. The second approach, factor-sensitivity measures, reflects changes for given predetermined underlying risk factors and provides information about the riskiness of a portfolio towards certain well-defined events (e.g. duration analysis). Among the disadvantages of this approach is its inability to analyse the aggregate sensitivity towards changes in different risk factors and thus cannot be used for determining capital adequacy decisions. Third, are measurements based on loss distributions such as VaR and variance methods, described as modern risk measures, which express loss distributions over a determined time horizon. The third approach is to some extent preferred because loss distributions facilitate aggregation of risks, reflect diversification effects and allow comparison of different portfolios (e.g. fixed-income port-folio with an equity-based portfolio). On the other hand, the efficient usage of such an approach is hindered by the historical data input, which is irrelevant when predicting future risk since market factors constantly change. Hence, scenario-based analysis, which is the final approach pre-sented, is recommended to predict future risks through simulating a number of possible risk-factor changes, and to measure the risk of a portfolio as the maximum loss under all scenarios. Such an approach is useful for meas-uring portfolio risks with a limited set of risk factors, but imposes a challenge when determining the appropriate set of scenarios.

Among the large variety of methods and approaches of risk measurement, VaR is considered a universal tool and is the most widely used methodology for quantifying dif-ferent types of risks; it facilitates the process of assigning risk limits to a bank's business units and, thus, the efficient allocation of capital (Saita 1999; Linsmeier and Pearson 2000). On the other hand, traditional/standard quan-tification methods, such as gap, duration and simulation models, among others, are being used to measure other risks. Consequently, within the context of this study, the different applications of the VaR model will be outlined first, followed by a general overview of the traditional risk assessment tools used to measure credit, market and opera-tional risks, as summarised in Table 4.1. The application of liquidity risk quantification models remains a challenge, yet after the latest wave of banking crises more focus has been directed towards liquidity risk measures. One way to instigate proper liquidity management is to adopt scenario-based analyses.

Basically, VaR measurement is the main foundation and the widely practised risk management technique of market

Table 4.1 *Risk measurement methods' application to risks*

Measurement method	Credit risk	Market risk	Operational risk
Value at Risk (VaR)	✓[a]	✓	✓
Expected Shortfall (ES)	✓	✓	✓
Credit ratings	✓		
Credit scoring	✓		
Gap analysis		✓	
Duration analysis		✓	
Sensitivity analysis[b]	✓	✓	✓
Stress testing[b]	✓	✓	✓
Scenario analysis[b]	✓	✓	✓
Qualitative methods (e.g. brain storming, professional experience)			✓

[a] The proposed credit Value-at-Risk methodologies proposed by the BIS as of 1998 are: CreditMetrics, KMV, CreditRisk+ and CreditPortfolioView.

[b] Methods of analysis that may be utilised for all types of risks, to back up or validate the results arising from other measurement methods.

risk quantification as it captures the multiple components of market risk. However, it is used for measuring credit risk as well as operational risk. VaR is defined as the maximum expected loss that might occur within a specified time period (e.g. one day or 10 days for market risk, and a year for credit and operational risk) at a specified probability/confidence level (common values are 0.95 or 0.99; McNeil *et al.* 2005). To compute VaR there are various techniques that can be used, such as the variance co-variance model, historical or Monte Carlo simulations and Riskmetrics (Saita 1999). Despite the time consumed and the high cost, the Monte Carlo simulation is one of the favoured methods to calculate VaR because it considers random draws on all distributions that represent price movements while considering different correlations among the variables. Another common method for calculating VaR is the Riskmetrics method developed by J. P. Morgan, which calculates the change in value within a 5 per cent confidence level over a one-day time period and assumes a normal distribution for market fluctuations (Marrison 2002; Pyle 1997).

Like other risk measurement models the VaR model has some possible drawbacks. It does not account for market risk generated by long-term operations, which in turn does not reflect management policies such as stop-loss limits designed to control cumulative losses (Dimakos and Aas 2004). Moreover, deficiencies of VaR calculation appear for confidence levels beyond 99 per cent (e.g. at $\alpha = 99.97\%$), where the confidence level is almost certain and does not account for possible errors in the model itself. It should be clear to risk managers that VaR is subject to model risk as it represents a simplified version of the economic world. Another drawback is that it neglects the effect of the market illiquidity that would occur if the maximum loss is realised (Long Term Capital Management is one example). Finally, similar to all loss distribution measures, it is difficult to determine a single optimal value for the time horizon and the confidence level to be used as risk parameters.

To overcome some of the deficiencies of the VaR approach, Expected Shortfall (ES)[3] is used by some risk management practitioners. Expected shortfall is interpreted as 'the expected loss that is incurred in the event that VaR is exceeded' (McNeil *et al.* 2005), in which the VaR is averaged over all confidence levels instead of measuring the expected loss at a specific confidence level. Additionally, scenario-based analyses, such as sensitivity analysis, stress testing and scenario analysis, are used to control the drawbacks associated with the VaR approach. These measurement techniques are widely used as common practices by the world's largest banks, such as UBS, Deutsche Bank, Société Générale and BNP Paribas.

Even with the applicability of measuring credit risk with the VaR model,[4] credit risk evaluation decisions are complex as a result of the various forms of risks involved and the huge volumes of raw data required for assessment. In addition are the difficulty of performing an *ex ante* analysis of credit risk, because it requires an assessment of the likelihood of default, possible recoveries under default, and it being almost impossible to calculate the effect of diversification at the portfolio level due to the difficulty of gathering data that clarifies the interdependencies between default events and different borrowers. Because of such difficulties, the BIS has always been concerned about credit risk assessment (credit risk being identified as the most important risk in a bank) and requires banks to have a thorough understanding of credit structures and the related exposures resulting from agreements between a bank and its customers; to establish well-identified credit limits; and to clearly set up credit policies in order to help maintain a sound credit assessment process (BCBS 2000b: 3; Marrison 2002: 231). Furthermore, the BIS disclosed that banks must adopt adequate analytical techniques that enable management to calculate credit exposures regularly and compare it to credit limits.

Credit risk is classified into Expected Losses (EL) that depend on the Probability of Defaults (PD) and Loss Given Default (LGD) assuming their independence, and Unexpected Losses (UL) that result from the variability of PDs and count for correlations among asset portfolios (Curcio and Gianfrancesco 2010). Traditionally, credit risk assessment[5] depends heavily on rating systems, where the efficiency of a rating system depends on its stability throughout a certain time horizon and its sensitivity towards changes that would affect the rating. Although internal and external credit rating systems are the most feasible methods to quantify credit risk, it is not sufficient to solely depend on such criteria because they do not provide an absolute measure of risk and are not designed to quantify the credit risk on a portfolio basis. Internal ratings are often used for risk reports, loan pricing and regulatory capital purposes, where such models are based on either PD and/or LGD. To provide an efficient assessment tool, rating models should be responsive to changing conditions, be transparent and consistent. Another common measure of credit risk are 'credit scoring models'; these are based on historical accounting ratios, which makes them non-responsive to changing market conditions (Heffernan 2005: 160; Kalapodas and Thomson 2006). One basic challenge facing credit risk quantification is the possible scarcity of required data, which – as mentioned before – is a specific problem when considering diversification effects on credit portfolios.

The BIS proposed different credit VaR methodologies within the 1998 Accord: CreditMetrics developed by J. P. Morgan, the structural approach suggested by the KMV model, CreditRisk+ proposed by Credit Suisse Financial Products, and finally the CreditPortfolioView recommended by McKinsey. The CreditMetrics approach analyses credit migrations; these are the movements from one credit quality to another (default also being considered), within a specified time horizon, usually set at one year. Likewise, the KMV model appears close to CreditMetrics but depends on the 'expected default frequency' for issuers rather than the historical transition probabilities provided by rating agencies. On the other hand, CreditRisk+ focuses only on defaults and assumes a Poisson distribution, while the CreditPortfolioView, still measuring only default risk, is a multi-period model based on macro-variables such as interest rate levels or economic growth rates. Even with these models, credit VaR measurement is accompanied by two challenges that hinder the application of credit VaR as compared to market VaR: first, the portfolio distribution is highly skewed and fat-tailed, unlike normal distributions with market risk, and second, it is much more complicated to quantify the portfolio effect as a result of credit diversification. Hence, calculating credit VaR requires a simulation of the full distribution of the credit portfolio value changes (Crouhy *et al.* 2000; Kalapodas and Thomson 2006). In 2006, Fatemi and Fooladi investigated the current practices of the largest US-based financial institutions. The results revealed that the majority of the credit risk models are mainly used to quantify counterparty default risk. Some banks are also concerned with counterparty migration risk and utilise models such as CreditMetrics for that purpose, while a few use internal credit risk assessment models. Results for similar studies should vary based on the geographical area and the implemented regulations.

On a different note, Crouhy *et al.* (2000) suggest that the 'ultimate framework' for credit risk analysis is one that integrates both market and credit risks rather than analysing credit risk independently. This approach is not supported by any of the proposed credit risk measurement models. As regards market risk measurement in banks, it has been noted that VaR is the widely used tool to quantify such risks. Nonetheless, traditional methods, such as gap analysis, duration analysis, sensitivity analysis, stress testing and scenario analysis, among others, are used to quantify risks resulting from market variations. Scenario analyses are indeed essential to supplement VaR estimates. A brief overview of such methods is provided below.

One major component of market risk in conventional

banks is interest rate risk that greatly affects profitability, and thus quantifying interest rate risk is central for conventional banks to enhance management decisions. Gap and duration-gap analyses are used to account for interest rate risk by measuring the sensitivity of cash flows towards market variations. Gap analysis requires the determination of the cash flows of assets and liabilities to assess the gap arising from re-pricing activities within a specified time interval such as a 30-day period. Duration analysis provides an overview of the average time required to recover invested funds and accounts for both on- and off-balance-sheet exposures. The drawbacks of these measurement models arise from their static nature that contradicts the dynamic nature of the banking business. This reveals the need for more accurate quantification methods to measure the effect of interest rate variations on earnings over different time horizons, such as simulation models (Santomero 1997).

Sensitivity analysis is one method used to quantify different components by measuring the effect of different market risk factors – such as interest rates, credit spreads, exchange rates, and equity or commodity prices – on the value of a portfolio. Sensitivity analysis is used when expected fluctuations in market risk factors are minimal; otherwise, stress testing is used to count for large risk-factor changes. Stress testing provides a clear measure of risk by revaluing a portfolio under multiple market factors – usually banks use around 100 factors – that affect the present value of the portfolio (Marrison 2002). Moreover, stress testing could be used to incorporate historical adverse market movements where it is assumed that future downturns will resemble historical events. The BIS acknowledges the importance of stress testing to disclose the setting of a bank's tolerance towards integrated risks (BCBS 2009: 24). Yet, it is also argued that stress testing is not accurate and does not clearly reflect problems, since it assumes zero or one correlations for different movements among risk factors that are not related to probabilities. Similar to stress testing, scenario analysis uses specific changes in market-risk factors to revalue a portfolio. Nevertheless, in scenario analysis the selection of changes in market-risk factors is subjective, usually in order to create a limited set of worst-case scenarios to match some historical crises, which constitutes a major drawback for scenario analysis (Marrison 2002).

The third important type of risks to be quantified in banks is operational risk. Operational risk quantification is a challenging topic as this risk is difficult to spot or identify and it resembles correlations with other risks. For instance, operational and credit risks are positively correlated and operational risk usually appears with credit risk (Dimakos and Aas 2004). Both qualitative and quantitative methods are used to account for operational risk, such as historical data, professional expertise and brain storming. Such methods make it possible to measure operational risk through evaluating the likelihood and cost of adverse events, where the frequency of events depends on the business/product volume. Gathering the required and sufficient data for assessment is one crucial factor that greatly affects the reliability of operational risk measurement. Despite the available methods of quantification, operational risk is integrated with complex banking operations and personnel, which makes it more difficult to analyse and quantify. Hence, the BIS constantly targets operational risk issues, among other risks, for adjustments that aim at a prudently regulated industry. Recent focus, however, has been on liquidity risk.

To measure operational risk, all the necessary information that aids the risk assessment process should first be gathered. Such information could be available through audit/regulatory/management reports and expert opinions, among others. The assessment of the gathered 'input' information serves as the second step, which can be done by classifying the operational risk into the main exposures, such as losses that stem from system failures or physical capital. When historical data are available, both the severity and probability of each of the sources of risks can be determined through quantitative measures; otherwise, when there is no reliable data, statistical data qualitative measures are put in place. In best cases, a numerical approach is recommended to combine between qualitative and quantitative measures. Before moving on to the third step, a summary report should be provided, including the assessed risk exposures and the factors considered during the assessment phase. Afterwards, the risk assessment process is reviewed by knowledgeable personnel, to ensure consistency in applying the framework. Finally, management actions based on the assessed and reported risks are required as a control method: for example, management can choose to withdraw from a certain business activity that exposes the bank to a very high risk, or transfer the risk to another party (e.g. insurance). In fact, such a process is applicable for measuring different types of risks.

4.2 Current practices in Islamic banks

Risk measurement is essential for Islamic banks to comply with international regulations and guidelines. Yet, a major challenge that faces Islamic banks is finding adequate and standardised risk measurement tools that meet the structure of the Islamic banking model and the accompanied financing activities, to facilitate the risk management process and support management decisions. The risk profile of Islamic banks comprises some risks that are similar to conventional banks. Hence, risk measurement in Islamic banks corresponds to that of conventional banks. Risks in Islamic banks, too, can either be measured on the overall bank level or on a division level, where integrating different risks imposes a challenge in terms of probability distributions, time horizon and correlations, as previously illustrated. Moreover, the different risk measurement approaches discussed earlier apply equally to the different banking models. Yet, applying any of the conventional measurement models to Islamic banks should incorporate a deep understanding of the nature of the Islamic banking contracts and the allocated/shared risks. A large set of conventional risk measurement methods is available for Islamic instruments; some simply fit the parallel risk structure, while others require further adjustments before being applied to the Islamic banking model. This section provides an overview of the methods outlined in the literature for measuring Islamic banks' risks.

Traditionally, banks use qualitative methods based on supervisory tools to analyse a bank's condition and present an adequate indication of the risk profile of the bank. Added to that, the risk position of a bank is currently assessed through quantitative measurements based on financial ratios and risk-based bank analysis. Hence, it is important for Islamic banks to integrate qualitative and quantitative measures when assessing a risk position. Yet, the use of quantitative methods represents a major challenge to the risk analysis process of Islamic banks. Based on Ariffin *et al.* (2009), the majority of Islamic banks do not use the advanced risk measurement approaches exploited by conventional banks, such as the VaR approach, simulation methods and RAROC. Having insufficient resources or systems explains why Islamic banks withdraw from using such technically advanced risk measurement methods. However, other traditional risk measures, such as maturity matching, gap analysis and ratings, are the most widely used measurement tools among Islamic banks.

In general, credit risk measurement requires an adequate understanding of the underlying credit structures to allow for a precise assessment of credit exposures. While credit risk assessment in conventional banks heavily depends on rating systems, specifically rating agencies, Islamic banks have limited access to external ratings. Therefore, in the absence of rating agencies, Islamic banks depend on internal rating systems, in which a client's creditworthiness is assessed through historical data – by evaluating past performance measures of the client's track record. During the assessment phase, restrictions on collaterals and penalties are considered among the factors that decrease recovery values and increase credit risk (Sundararajan 2007; Iqbal and Mirakhor 2007). Ahmed and Khan (2007) suggest that applying internal rating systems, in which risk weights are assigned for all assets separately, is essential in filling the risk management gaps in Islamic banks. Furthermore, Akkizidis and Khandelwal (2008) demonstrate that, after determining the final ratings (e.g. very good, good, satisfactory, sufficient, insufficient), they should then be translated into risk values (i.e. low, below average, average, above average, high) corresponding to a scale of grades designed to facilitate the assessment process. Initiating such systems in Islamic banks will pave the way towards more sophisticated risk measurement tools and enhance the assessments of regulatory authorities and rating agencies.

Sundararajan (2007) discusses credit risk management in Islamic banks in view of the three required estimates (based on Basel II) to evaluate loans, namely: probability of default (PD), exposure at default (EAD) and loss given default (LGD). Sundararajan suggests that since the LGD depends on the value of the collateral, LGD in Islamic banks will theoretically be higher than in conventional counterparties because of the *Shari'ah* restrictions imposed on requesting collaterals. Furthermore, specifically in Islamic financing contracts, EAD for *murabaha* and *salam* contracts amounts to the nominal value of the loan, whereas EAD for *istisna'a* and *ijara* depends on other facility specific factors, such as relevant environmental or market factors.

A large set of risk measurement techniques is available for quantifying market risk, similar to those presented earlier for conventional banks. For instance, Islamic banks tend to use liquidity gap to measure the market risk between assets and liabilities at various maturities. However, VaR methodology is a better measure since it captures maximum losses that might occur at certain probabilities. It is recommended that commodity price risk should not only be treated as part of market risk, but also be added to credit risk since it is embedded in the contracts, and should be accounted for individually when pricing or monitoring the price risk for each contract or a portfolio of contracts. Further, unexpected losses of investment deposits can be assessed by calculating the variability of the rate of return attributable to IAHs under alternative scenarios of PER and IRR. As regards liquidity in Islamic banks, it is simply accounted for by measuring current assets to current liabilities or current assets to total assets (Sundararajan 2007).

Freeland and Friedman (2007: 215–22) acknowledge that while managing and measuring operational risks are relatively new concepts, and the associated methods and techniques are still under development, there is a significantly growing trend towards carefully monitoring such risks under complex financial systems. Hence, Islamic banks opt to measure operational risk via one of the three measurement methods provided by Basel II: Basic Indicator Approach (BIA), Standardised Approach (SA) or Advanced

Measurement Approach (AMA). The BIA entails 15 per cent of gross income to be accounted for by operational risks within the capital, which could be misleading in the case of Islamic banks since a large volume of transactions in commodities that give rise to operational risk will not be captured by gross income. The SA stipulates a percentage that varies between 12 and 18 per cent, based on the business line: 18 per cent for corporate finance, trading and sales, settlement and payments, 15 per cent for commercial banking and agency services, and 12 per cent for retail banking and asset management. Even though the SA requires some adaptation to the characteristics of Islamic banks it is believed to be a better-suited method for the measurement of Islamic banks' operational risk (Archer and Haron 2007). However, the IFSB proposed that, while the SA was allowed, Islamic banks should instead adopt the BIA (Moore 2007: 237–46). Moreover, operational risk can be measured by calculating the Profit at Risk (PaR), which uses a confidence interval (Z_α) to compute the variability of net returns (σ_p) at a holding period (T): $PaR = Z_\alpha \, \sigma_p \sqrt{T}$ (Sundararajan 2007). On a different note, in order to reach realistic conclusions with regard to operational risk measurement, Islamic banks should cooperate and give priority to measuring operational risk and providing an aggregate pool of information through recording loss events globally for all Islamic banks.

From the above, it can be concluded that risk measurement in Islamic banks is an underdeveloped area of research. It is essential to employ adequate risk measurement and disclosure methods, should Islamic banks opt for adopting the new Basel Capital Accord. Bessis (2002) stipulates that modelling risks is the only way to quantify them, as risk models measure risks for evaluation and allow a tracing-back system for control purposes. Consequently, applications of modern methods for credit and overall banking risk measurement should be adapted to fit Islamic banks. Such measurement approaches will recognise the mix of risks in Islamic products, ensure a better pricing for the various Islamic financial contracts, provide satisfactory returns to IAHs, and sustain an adequate level of capital with an effective allocation-per-risk profile. However, based on Akkizidis and Khandelwal (2008), there is a level of uncertainty associated with building quantitative risk measurement models, hence, Islamic banks should have a clear and validated process when constructing similar quantitative models. The process starts with identifying the usability and accessibility of available historical data. Afterwards, the data should be simulated for analysis, the model methodology should be determined, and the parameters of the model should be identified. Finally, it should be validated via qualitative and quantitative methods, where examples of quantitative validation methods are back-testing and stress testing. Despite the importance of historical data and information, Islamic banks currently suffer from a scarcity of databases, as accumulating and disclosing information relevant to counterparties, as well as the unification of data, remains a challenge. This clearly hinders the development and application of quantitative measurement models.

To facilitate quantitative and effective risk management in Islamic financial institutions, an informational database must be initiated among Islamic banks, unified accounting and reporting standards should be followed and strengthened, and risk measurement should include aggregate risk measures. Specifically, informational data is critical for risk measurement, which includes financial-ratio analysis that depends on the timeliness, completeness and accuracy of data inputs. Therefore, transparency and consistency of financial figures is essential for an effective analysis of risks. However, only a few institutions, banks and regulatory bodies follow the unified accounting and reporting standards issued by the AAOIFI that clarify the methods of income and loss recognition. Such standards – unified accounting and reporting standards – should be implemented by, at least, the main market players so that other Islamic banks automatically apply them as a response to market forces (Ahmed and Khan 2007).

Finally, Grais and Kulathunga (2007) suggest that Islamic banks should work together to pool sufficient information and enhance the process of risk management in practice and theory. Improvements in risk management will facilitate Islamic banks' ability to assess capital requirements and hence use available resources efficiently. Further discussion on risk measurement techniques follow in the next section, elaborating on the appropriate risk assessment models for each risk.

4.3 Developing risk assessment in Islamic banks

In the previous section it has been emphasised that Islamic banks should utilise both qualitative and quantitative risk measurement methods, and the challenges faced by Islamic banks in quantifying risks have been presented. Quantitative risk measures represent a main challenge to Islamic banks, as a lack of sufficient resources, data and systems hinders Islamic banks to use the advanced measurement models utilised by conventional banks. The majority of Islamic banks are relatively small in size and thus usually lack sufficient resources to adequately quantify risks and are not able to afford adopting advanced systems. Moreover, the lack of supporting historical data greatly contributes to the quantification challenge; since not all Islamic banks follow a unified reporting system, the reported data will either be incomplete or inconsistent. Thus, if data is available it requires great efforts to unify it for systematic use. Accumulating a comprehensive set of data is indispensable since risk measurement should include aggregate risks. Accordingly, as Sundararajan (2007) and Greuning and Iqbal (2007), among others, suggest, an informational database must be initiated among the Islamic banking industry, in which unified accounting and reporting standards are ensured and strengthened to facilitate quantitative and effective risk measurement in Islamic financial institutions.

Consequently, the main problem of a lack of sufficient data to measure risks must be resolved as a preliminary step to developing risk measurement in Islamic banks. In response to that challenge a risk reporting system must be established and adopted by Islamic banks. As Islamic banks are faced by a mix of risks that are identified first on the contractual level and then on the overall business level, following a system to identify and report the associated risks on each of the levels is recommended. Accordingly, adopting a coded risk matrix is an easy approach that would facilitate risk analysis and help identify risk correlations. Nevertheless, common definitions of risks should be ensured and cooperation should be given priority to provide an aggregate pool of information by recording risk events. The presented coding system recognises the combination of different risk factors for each contract, which will facilitate accumulation of market data based on a unified reporting system. Later, the volatility of these risk factors and their sensitivity to different market conditions can be measured using different risk quantification models. The importance of pooling information for measurement and management issues must be emphasised.

As shown in Table 4.2, each bank risk is codified using three letters and two numbers. The first letter represents the first letter of the main risk category, the middle letter is

Table 4.2 *Risks coding system*

Type of risk			
Main category	**Sub category**	**Code**	*Murabaha* (01)
Credit risk		CRX	CRX01
Market risk	Commodity/ asset price	MRC	
	Residual value	MRR	
	Mark up	MRM	MRM01
	FX	MRF	MRF01
	Equity	MRE	
Equity investment		ERX	
Liquidity risk	Fund-raising	LRF	LRF01
	Trading	LRT	
Operational risk (Internal operational risk)	Systems	ORS	ORS01
	People	ORP	ORP01
	Physical capital	ORC	ORC01
	Legal	ORL	ORL01
	Shari'ah	ORS	ORS01
Business risk (External operational risk)	Systemic	BRS	
	Political	BRP	
	DCR	BRD	
	Rate of return	BRR	
	Withdrawal	BRW	

constantly stated as 'R' as an indicator for the word risk, and the third letter stands for the first letter of the subcategory of the risk (risk categories and subcategories are provided on page 35 of this book). For example, commodity price risk, which is a subcategory of market risk, is coded as MRC: M stands for market, R is for risk, and C denotes commodity

Sources of risk				
Products				
Ijara (02)	*Salam* (03)	*Istisna'a* (04)	*Mudaraba* (05)	**Overall** (06)
CRX02	CRX03	CRX04	CRX05	CRX06
MRC02	MRC03	MRC04		
MRR02 MRM02 MRF02	MRF03	MRF04	MRF05	MRF06 MRE06
			ERX05	
LRF02	LRF03	LRF04	LRF05	LRF06 LRT06
ORS02	ORS03	ORS04	ORS05	ORS06
ORP02	ORP03	ORP04	ORP05	ORP06
ORC02	ORC03	ORC04		ORC06
ORL02	ORL03	ORL04	ORL05	ORL06
ORS02	ORS03	ORS04	ORS05	ORS06
				BRS06 BRP06 BRD06 BRR06 BRW06

price risk. Similarly, systems risk, which is a subcategory of operational risk, is coded as ORS, and so forth for the entire risk map. For risks that do not hold subcategories, such as credit risk, the letter for the subcategory is replaced by X. As such, credit risk and equity investment risk are coded as CRX and ERX, respectively.

Furthermore, to facilitate the risk analysis, mitigation and review, the sources of risks on both contractual and overall levels are given numbers. Each product/contract as well as the overall risk level are given numbers starting from 01 going up to 06 for *murabaha, ijara, salam, istisna'a, mudaraba* and the overall level, respectively. Accordingly, the source of credit risk in a *murabaha* contract is coded as CRX01, whereas it is coded as CRX02 in an *ijara* contract. Elaborating further, one of the risks underlying a *murabaha* contract is identified as credit risk (CRX01), where the 01 in this code refers to the *murabaha* contract. This means that the code (CRX01) refers to credit risk, identified as CRX, underlying the *murabaha* contract, denoted by 01. Similarly, market risks under *murabaha* contracts are referred to as MRM01 for mark-up risk and MRF01 for foreign exchange risk, whereas liquidity fund-raising risk is coded as LRF01, and so forth.

This coding system is utilised for the risk analysis and mitigation processes within the relevant chapters. Moreover, it is recommended to be embedded within the risk management process of Islamic banks to facilitate risk reporting and review. This aims at facilitating the development of an adequate reporting system throughout Islamic banks.

Once a risk database is created, different approaches for managing risks can be used. Looking at the widely practised risk assessment methodologies available to banks, the risk measurement methods applicable to Islamic banks are identified for each risk. Yet, before exploring the assessment methods for each risk, it is important to remember some points that arise mainly due to the specific nature of Islamic banks and the resulting changes in the risk map. While analysing Islamic banks' risks, the unique mix of risks must be recognised, the Islamic finance facilities should be properly priced, and the risk-return results for IAHs must be disclosed and managed appropriately. Moreover, the adequacy of capital and its effective allocation based on the risk-return analysis of the business units ought to be ensured. This suggests the importance of assessing risks based on a risk-return analysis, in order to adequately evaluate the risks taken by the bank and manage them accordingly. Furthermore, two points regarding the use of benchmarks within an Islamic finance context and the availability of historical data as a major obstacle towards risk quantification should be clarified.

It is known that Islamic principles agree with conventional finance in terms of the risk-return principle, highlighted by Markowitz (1991), where an increase in the expected return can only be realised with an increase in the portfolio risk. However, Islamic finance does not recognise the concept of a risk-free rate of return, as no extra return can be realised for free based on Islamic principles. In principle, the absence of a risk-free return distorts the concept of measuring risks relevant to Islamic banks based on a risk-free benchmark as utilised in conventional finance theories. However, based on rulings by *Shari'ah* experts, such as Abdulazeem Abozaid, Mohamed Al-Beltagy and Habib Ahmed, it is not against Islamic principles to price products or measure risks based on a conventional benchmark whether it be a risk-free or risky benchmark. Moreover, the AAOIFI (2008b) stipulates the use of 'indices for guidance in operations that relate to real transactions is permissible in *Shari'ah*', where indices may be used to identify the magnitude and pattern of market changes, evaluate performance relatively and forecast future market changes, among others. Hence, an index like LIBOR is used to determine the profit of *murabaha* contracts, determine the variable rent in *ijara* contracts and act as benchmark for comparisons.

The risk measurement models most suitable to each risk can now be discussed. Table 4.3 summarises the risk

Table 4.3 *Measurement models for Islamic bank risks*

Type of risk			Var	Credit	Credit
Main category	Sub category	Code	(ES)	ratings	scoring
Credit risk		CRX	✓	✓	✓
Market risk	Commodity/ price	MRC	✓		
	Residual value	MRR			
	Mark up	MRM	✓		
	FX	MRF	✓		
	Equity	MRE	✓		
Equity investment		ERX			
Liquidity risk	Fund- raising	LRF			
	Trading	LRT			
Operational risk	Systems	ORS			
	People	ORP			
	Physical capital	ORC			
	Legal	ORL			
	Shari'ah	ORS			
Business risk	Systemic	BRS			
	Political	BRP			
	DCR	BRD			
	Rate of return	BRR	✓		
	Withdrawal	BRW			

Measurement method				
Gap analysis	Duration analysis	Scenario-based analysis	Qualitative method	Other methods
		✓	✓	
		✓		
				Accounting methods
	✓	✓		
		✓		
		✓		
		✓		SWOT[a]
✓		✓		
		✓		
		✓	✓	
		✓	✓	
		✓	✓	
		✓	✓	
		✓	✓	
		✓		
		✓		
		✓		
✓	✓	✓		
		✓		

[a] Strengths, Weaknesses, Opportunities and Threats analysis.

measurement models that can be utilised by Islamic banks for each set of risks. Each of these methods has been briefly explained earlier. Credit risk (CRX) may be measured using VaR, credit ratings systems, credit scoring, scenario-based analysis, and qualitative methods such as evaluating the creditworthiness of clients. On the other hand, market risk factors have a more limited set of measurement methods, where VaR and scenario-based analysis could be utilised for the different market risk factors, with the exception of residual risk (MRR). Residual risk may be calculated using accounting and mathematical methods. Moreover, duration analysis can only be utilised for quantifying mark-up risk (MRM), since it resembles interest rate risk. Furthermore, equity investment risk, operational risks, liquidity risks and business risks may be equally evaluated using scenario-based analysis. Yet, fund-raising liquidity risk (LRF) may also be accounted for by identifying liquidity gaps. Rate-of-return risk (BRR) may be calculated with gap analysis, duration analysis or the VaR approach, since BRR risk has similar characteristics to interest rate risk. Finally, operational risks are instead assessed via qualitative methods.

Pyle (1997: 12) identifies the main components of credit risk assessment that should be considered during evaluation decisions as probabilities of default, recoveries under default and deterioration in payments. Similarly, Curcio and Gianfrancesco (2010) sum up the factors that influence loan-pricing decisions in banks, in which risk is a main element, as being related to counterparties (such as guarantees and loan maturities), internal factors determined by the bank (e.g. degree of diversification or cost of funding) and institutional/external factors. The last factor may relate to market elements, such as the availability of an active secondary market, or to regulatory requirements. These factors should be considered in the assessment of credit risk for each individual contract and then accumulated on a portfolio and/or divisional level.

The VaR (viewed as the economic capital) approach is a widely practised risk measurement tool for various reasons. It also qualifies for use in identifying adequate capital. Based on the proposed classification of risks for Islamic banks, the VaR approach may be utilised for credit risk (CRX), market risks (with the exception of the residual value risk – MRR) and rate-of return-risk (BRR). The application of VaR to the mentioned Islamic bank risks resembles its application to conventional bank risks. That is, the risk measure is applied to risks of a similar nature in both banking systems, despite witnessing a different classification in some cases, such as with market risks. Thus, the various techniques used to compute VaR are equally applicable for Islamic banks, provided that the required data inputs are made available.[6]

To compute credit VaR two types of losses are identified: an expected loss (EL) that is covered by provisions and unexpected loss (UL) that lies beyond the level of the identified EL. According to Akkizidis and Khandelwal (2008), EL is simply calculated by multiplying the probability of default (PD), loss given default (LGD) and exposure at default (EAD), whereas the calculation of UL requires more advanced statistical methods. Finally, in a portfolio of credits, the effect of correlation should be considered for the estimation of the LGD (assets correlation) and the PD (default correlation). It should be noted that the time horizon considered when calculating VaR for long-term financial contracts should be extended, unlike when short- or medium-term contracts are evaluated.

Credit rating is a common method used for analysing credit risks and is recommended for Islamic banks by Ahmed and Khan (2007) and Akkizidis and Khandelwal

(2008), among others. Credit rating agencies play an important role in credit risk assessment, but Islamic banks have limited access to external rating agencies. Hence, Islamic banks mainly depend on an internal rating system in assessing their clients' creditworthiness. Islamic banks mainly use credit scoring for evaluating credit risk, as more sophisticated measurement models do not fit with the current operational Islamic bank model. It is claimed that Islamic banks, being conservative with their business model and relatively small in size, do not need and cannot afford to adopt more advanced risk measurement models. Moreover, the International Islamic Rating Agency (IIRA) has been established in Bahrain, to provide credit ratings of public and private issuers of credit instruments. In addition it assesses the *Shari'ah* compliance of financial institutions and financial instruments, through a *Shari'ah* board. Yet, it remains a requirement to have credit rating agencies in different countries offering Islamic financial services to facilitate the process of selecting counterparties to Islamic banks (Chapra 2007: 331).

Finally, the mix of credit risk and correlations involved within the different financial contracts should be considered when determining the aggregate credit risk, as some instruments are known to have higher risks than others, which will eventually affect the overall credit risk of the bank. Furthermore, it is recommended to back credit risk assessment by assuming various default probabilities based on a scenario analysis and calculating the expected and unexpected losses accordingly. This is intended to increase the validity of the calculated credit risk and enhance the bank's risk management position.

Market risk, classified into commodity price risk (MRC), mark-up risk (MRM), currency risk (MRF) and equity risk (MRE) can equally be evaluated with the VaR approach.

However, given a certain probability and specified time, the risk factor varies for each of these risks. As such, the market input factors will be commodity prices for commodity-price risk, market interest rates for mark-up risk, currency prices for foreign-exchange risk and equity prices for equity risk. Also, the mix of risks per contract should be recognised: not all market risks are inherent in each financial contract, as risks vary on the individual contractual level. For instance, a *murabaha* contract constitutes only MRM and MRF risks, while an *ijara* contract includes four components of market risks: MRC, MRR, MRM and MRF. Accordingly, to facilitate the quantification of market risks, a detailed unified database of historical data should be maintained. Once historical data for each market risk factor for every financial contract is made available, the computation of market VaR will be easy to implement. It is worth noting that Islamic banks do not differ completely from conventional banks in terms of commodity price risk, since, as acknowledged by Crouhy *et al.* (2001) and Bessis (2002), there is a commodity-price risk element embedded within market risk in conventional banks, but it is more complex to measure than other market risk elements. However, since Islamic banks' products are asset-backed, the problem of the commodity/ asset price risk appears to be more complex than in their conventional counterparts.

Even though mark-up risk (MRM) has the same features as interest rate risk, it is not recommended to use gap analysis for measuring MRM risk. Since gap analysis requires the determination of the cash flows of assets and liabilities to assess the gap arising from re-pricing activities, such a measurement will not be accurate if used for mark-up risks in Islamic banks. This is because mark-up risk only appears in *murabaha* and *ijara* contracts on the assets side; both contracts do not normally exist on the liabilities side of an

Islamic bank. To the contrary, duration analysis is suitable as an MRM risk measure, as it provides an overview of the average time required to recover an investment, and thus a measure of the underlying risk. Nevertheless, simulation/scenario-based quantification methods are used for market risk analysis to account for the dynamic nature of the various market risk factors, which is not recognised by gap analysis.

Finally, it is worth noting that, on the contractual level, the method used for pricing each financial contract should be clearly identified to allow an adequate analysis of market risks. Such a clarification is essential as the pricing method affects the underlying risk factors, which in turn affect the risk assessment. For example, in cases of *murabaha*, the prices of contracts are based on mark-up rates, and market risk will be calculated by setting the future cash flows with consideration given to possible market interest-rate changes. On the other hand, in cases of product-deferred instruments, such as *salam*, where the price is determined based on the commodity/asset price, market risk will be calculated based on possible market price fluctuations for the underlying commodity/asset. Hence, it is essential to clearly capture the factors used to price the different financial contracts to produce an adequate analysis of the underlying risks.

Equity investment risk (ERX) can basically be analysed by setting different scenarios for possible cash-flow distortions or capital impairments within the equity investments; for example, by assuming different situations of profits, losses and break-even scenarios at different stages (years) of the invested project. In addition, Mohamed and Kayed (2007) suggest a framework for analysing equity investment risks that includes performing a SWOT analysis, fundamental analysis and adequate measurement of risks.

The SWOT analysis should enable the investor to estimate future performance through evaluating the strengths (internal potential capability to develop and grow), weaknesses (limitations), opportunities (external growth chances) and threats (external events that may cause negative effect) of a certain investment. Fundamental analysis is based on analysing the financial position of an investment as well as its surrounding factors (i.e. industry, economic factors, among others), hence, forecasting future cash flows. Finally, measuring risk by calculating the VaR, as the most frequently used methodology, is suggested for its simplicity. Such a framework can be adapted specifically to PLS agreements in an Islamic bank.

Measuring liquidity risk is an equally challenging topic for both conventional and Islamic banks. Within this context, suggestions for liquidity risk measurement are presented. In theory, a bank's liquidity position is judged by calculating liquidity financial ratios, such as dividing Current Assets (CA) by Current Liabilities (CL) or CA by Total Assets (TA). In general, higher ratios reflect a better liquidity position for the bank. Yet, it is necessary to consider the fact that maintaining higher liquidity ratios has a negative impact on a bank's profit. Another approach to analyse liquidity risk is to calculate the maturity gaps, which provide an indicator for liquidity risk. When measuring a bank's maturity gap, different scenarios could be utilised to identify the bank's liquidity position under certain projections.

Once risks are analysed, mitigation methods should be identified for each risk and on the overall bank level. There are different general mitigation strategies that are explained in the next chapter. Moreover, for each Islamic financing mode there are some mitigation methods that are identified and indicated as suitable for each contract; contractual mitigation methods would vary from one contract to another.

The next chapter explores the various mitigation methods for Islamic banks.

Notes

1. For more details about the CAMELS rating system refer to R. Sahajwala and P. Van den Bergh (2000), *Supervisory Risk Assessment and Early Warning Systems*. Basel: Bank for International Settlements (BIS).
2. To solve this problem the Basel Accord uses a one-year time horizon when integrating different risks (Dimakos and Aas 2004).
3. For more details about ES measurement refer to chapter 6 in A. McNeil, R. Frey and P. Embrechts (2005), *Quantitative Risk Management: Concepts, Techniques and Tools*. Princeton, NJ: Princeton University Press.
4. Refer to E. Kalapodas and M. Thomson (2006), 'Credit risk assessment: a challenge for financial institutions', *IMA Journal of Mathematics*, 17: 25–46.
5. For further reading about credit risk measurement models, refer to chapter 8 in McNeil *et al. Quantitative Risk Management.*
6. See section 4.1 for a review of the techniques used to compute VaR.

CHAPTER 5
RISK MITIGATION

The third step in a risk management process is mitigation of risks. This chapter elaborates on the risk mitigation strategies for Islamic banks. Generally, risk mitigation strategies are divided into active and passive strategies based on the structure of the risk, which is composed of the risk occurrence probability and its accompanied consequences. Passive strategies are those which do not change the consequence or probability of the risk; active strategies normally have an effect on the consequence and probability of the risk. Passive strategies are basically divided into risk financing and risk transfer, while active strategies include risk avoidance, reduction and diversification. Following the two-level identification approach, Islamic banks' mitigation strategies should be conducted on two levels, the overall bank level and the contract level. On the contract level, mitigation methods applicable for each financial contract are identified by examining the AAOIFI disclosed accounting and *Shari'ah* standards. Within the requirements specified for each contract, the AAOIFI presents mitigation methods that can be used to manage the different risks per contract. For example, in a *murabaha* contract, it is stipulated that the bank may ask the client to pay *hamish jiddiyyah* (security deposit) before proceeding to buy the requested asset/good. This payment is considered as a down payment requested by the bank to make sure that the client will fulfil his promise in purchasing the ordered good/asset. This mitigates the bank's credit risk, specifically in being left with the goods purchased on behalf of the client, as it minimises the risk that the client may refuse to conclude the *murabaha* transaction. In the same way, each element specified in each Islamic financial contract is examined and linked to a suitable contractual mitigation method.

5.1 Mitigating overall risks

After risks are successfully analysed, a bank identifies the appropriate mitigation strategies that would minimise its overall risk position. Risk mitigation is an important step in the risk management process that is practised by all financial institutions and is sometimes referred to as risk control. During this stage, different strategies are used to mitigate the risks previously identified and assessed. Similar to Islamic banks' risk measurement, risk mitigation methods, specifically *Shari'ah*-based, also remain a challenging topic for Islamic banks. At the core of the Islamic bank model, there are some characteristics that are specifically useful to risk mitigation. First, Islamic banking products are backed by assets and, hence, this should minimise exposure to credit risks, which makes, for example, *sukuk* (Islamic bonds) less risky than conventional bonds (Fiennes 2007). Second, the profit and loss nature of the bank model implies that some risks should be borne by investors, resulting in a lower risk to the bank. Finally, *Shari'ah* principles act as a risk moderator, because they rule that each contract must be drawn up in clear terms without concealing any item or aspect of the contract (complete transparency) and avoiding excessive unnecessary risks. Otherwise, the contract will involve *gharar* and therefore be void (Akkizidis and Khandelwal 2007: 12).

On the down side, Islamic banks in practice deviate from theory, which gives rise to more risks that need further mitigation strategies. The unique mix of risks of the products at each stage of the contract heightens the need to cover some of the associated risks. New risks stem from the PLS nature of Islamic banks, such as displaced commercial risks, and require Islamic banks to be even more transparent than their conventional counterparts in reporting risk information. Finally, some conventional risk mitigation instruments are not allowed in Islamic banks because they do not comply with the *Shari'ah* principles. Grais and Kulathunga (2007) suggest that the prohibition of *gharar* is the main reason that restricts the use of some conventional finance hedging instruments.

Another reason that can be added to considering Islamic risk mitigation a challenge is that risks intermingle and interchange from one stage to another throughout an Islamic finance transaction. Furthermore, deficiencies within the institutions and instruments magnify the risks and increase the difficulty of their management, especially for operational risks (Ahmed and Khan 2007). Therefore, risk mitigation in Islamic banks is a new area that clearly requires the development of innovative *Shari'ah*-based risk mitigation techniques.

Such a demand stresses the need to embrace the knowledge of both *Shari'ah* principles and modern risk management techniques. It should be made clear that hedging risks in Islamic banks is a desirable act under *Shari'ah* principles, in the sense that *Shari'ah* aims to neutralise the risks involved in financial activities. Standard techniques of risk mitigation, such as risk reporting, internal and external audit, can be used for Islamic banks but other more advanced/technical tools need to be adapted to the specific nature of Islamic banks. This chapter provides an insight into the possible risk mitigation strategies applicable to Islamic banks.

In general, risk mitigation strategies could be divided into active and passive based on the risk structure, which is composed of the risk occurrence probability and its accompanying consequences. Passive strategies are those which do not change the consequence or the probability of the risk. To the contrary, active strategies normally affect the consequence and the probability of the risk. Active strategies include risk avoidance, risk reduction and risk diversification, while passive strategies are basically divided into risk financing and risk transfer (Schierenbeck and Lister 2002: 353).

The first active risk mitigation strategy – risk avoidance – generally refers to avoiding a certain risk by eliminating the probability of its occurrence (e.g. refusing a specific loan obligation). This is often a preferred strategy when the severity of loss is high. The second strategy – risk reduction – refers to minimising the probability of the consequences (severity) of an event (e.g. putting in fire alarms, more guards to reduce theft, training employees; (Dorfman 2005: 52–4). The third active strategy – risk diversification – involves diversifying the events of uncertainty and thus minimising the end result of the risk (e.g. by investing in different sectors within a bank's portfolio of assets).

Among the active strategies used by Islamic banks is risk avoidance or elimination. This is brought about through contractual risk mitigation, setting parallel contracts, netting on balance sheet or immunisation. Having the appropriate contractual agreements in place between counterparties, where different items, requirements and specifications are clearly identified, acts as a risk control technique that avoids *gharar* (contractual uncertainty). For instance, in some Islamic finance contracts *Shari'ah* scholars allow a penalty clause (*band al-jazaa*) as a method to overcome counterparty risk, such as delivering unqualified assets or deferred payments. In other contracts, a discount can be offered on the remaining mark-up to promote early settlement. In addition, one common tool that is used to manage market risk is that of constructing two parallel contracts, such as *salam* and parallel *salam*, where the latter acts as the hedging tool (Ahmed and Khan 2007). The other two risk avoidance strategies, netting on the balance sheet, which implies matching mutual financial obligations to net positions, and immunisation through setting hedging strategies, are suggested but are not easily put into practice and so require further consideration. Another common risk avoidance strategy practised by Islamic banks is to avoid engaging in risky contracts such as profit and loss sharing (PLS) contracts, represented by *mudaraba* and *musharaka*, as by nature such contracts are said to hold higher risks than other Islamic finance contracts.

With regard to the passive strategies, risk financing within a bank means that the consequences of the risk will be borne by the bank. Dorfman (2005) suggests that risk financing is a desired strategy when the consequences and the probability of loss are relatively low. However, based on the BIS, banks finance risks for both expected and unexpected losses, regardless of the severity of the loss. Expected losses are basically covered by provisions, while a bank's capital acts as a cushion to cover unexpected losses (BCBS 2006a). Nevertheless, when a bank's available capital fails to absorb such losses, the bank is said to be facing solvency risk that is said to be equivalent to default risk. The other form of passive mitigation strategy is risk transfer, which is subdivided into traditional and alternative risk transfer methods. Traditional risk transfer methods refer to transferring risk to another party, such as an insurance company or financial derivatives (e.g. financial options, swaps and futures). Alternative risk transfer methods refer to managing risks through financial contracts, such as risk bonds, which is defined as a net debt service referred to the damage where interest rates and principal are reduced respective to the loss (if occurred) (Schierenbeck and Lister 2002).

Collaterals, guarantees and parallel contracts are risk transfer methods commonly utilised in Islamic banks. Derivatives are the most common method of risk transfer used by conventional banks; however, the use of derivative instruments, such as credit derivatives, is restricted by *Shari'ah* law because they involve *riba* and *gharar*. That most of the traded derivative instruments involve no intention of making or taking delivery of the underlying assets is a clear feature that is embedded in such contracts, which is also unacceptable to *Shari'ah* law (Ariffin *et al.* 2009). Yet, some *Shari'ah*-compliant derivatives have recently been introduced to the market and are used by a few Islamic financial institutions. Whether such instruments should be widely accepted in the Islamic financial market requires further research. Ahmed and Khan (2007) propose some risk transfer tools that can be used by Islamic banks: examples are swaps, *salam* and commodity futures. (These tools are further elaborated in a following section.) Furthermore, as was previously explained, some bank risks, specifically the inseparable or complex risks, can be absorbed or managed within the bank. Islamic banks have such risks that can be mitigated through loan loss reserves and adequate allocation of capital.

Specifically in banks, risks that are not borne by the bank could be transferred, avoided or managed at the bank level (e.g. reduction and diversification, among others). Yet, managing risk at the bank level must be accompanied by a justifiable return, where it should be ensured that the mitigation costs do not exceed the managed risks; otherwise it is more prudent to transfer the risk (Allen and Santomero 1998; Al-Tamimi and Al-Mazrooei 2007). Santomero (1997: 4) sums up two cases where risk should be managed at the bank level: the first is when risks are too complex to communicate to a third party and the second is when holding the risky assets is central to the banking business, as with the case of credit risk. It is worth noting that the transference of complicated risks, which were not easy to understand, to the financial market was one of the factors that escalated the sub-prime crisis.

Ahmed and Khan (2007) state that Islamic banks basically apply three mitigation strategies – risk avoidance, risk transfer and risk absorption – as depicted in Figure 5.1. Similarly, Mohamed and Kayed (2007) add three risk mitigation strategies. The first is risk retention, which is mainly based on accepting the risk as part of an investment or a business without conducting any action to reduce or eliminate the risk. This may be because the risk consequence is low or it is critical for the core business and cannot be eliminated. The second strategy is risk reduction, where the risk consequence or likelihood is minimised to an acceptable level, and finally, there is diversifying investments and funds, which leads to risk diversification.

At the overall level, banks employ risk-related policies and standards in order to control risks. In addition, enforcement of institutional risk limits must be ensured as well as regular risk reporting to key decision makers (Meyer 2000). As banking involves a large variety of risks, different risk mitigation strategies are implemented within the bank based on the type of business activity and its underlying risk; for example, it is common for banks to manage

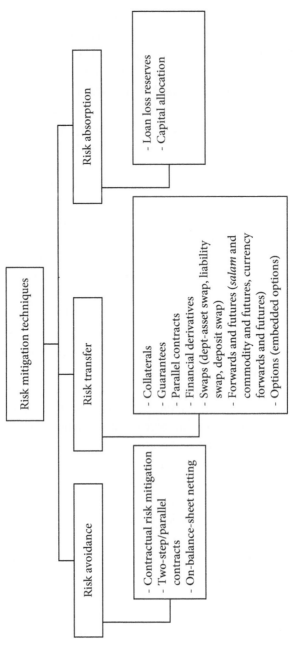

Figure 5.1 *Risk mitigation techniques in Islamic banks. Source: based on Ahmed and Khan (2007)*

market risks through hedging in the derivatives market. Other risks, such as operational, legal, regulatory, reputational and environmental risks, should be accounted for at the senior management level of the bank (Santomero 1997: 20–1). Below, the common risk mitigation strategies for credit, market and liquidity risks are elaborated.

In general, ensuring adequate controls over credit risk is one of the main elements of establishing a comprehensive credit risk management programme as recommended by the BIS (BCBS 2009: 11). Banks mainly cover credit risk by four common methods. These are that the bank should request collaterals, identify adequate provisions and reserves, apply internal rating systems and ensure that effective monitoring procedures are in place. Additionally, settlement limits should also be determined to minimise the bank's losses in case a client defaults midway. A proper assessment of loan obligations facilitates the process of determining the required collaterals to cover possible defaults, while having an adequate amount of provisions and reserves protects the bank against further estimated losses. It is worth noting that banks use internal ratings as well as external ratings, when available, to assure the creditworthiness of borrowers. An internal rating system categorises credits into various classes of risk, and its degree of sophistication should depend on the bank's business complexity. On the other hand, external ratings reflect changes in expected loan losses to give some comfort regarding asset quality. Finally, to ensure an efficient control over credit risk, consistent reporting and monitoring of all lending facilities (assets) should be enforced, to assure that no credit exposures exceed the predetermined credit risk limits, on both the portfolio and individual levels (BCBS 2000).

Specifically, in Islamic banks credit risk management is perceived to be more complicated than in their conventional counterparts because of the possible leniency towards default and delay in payments. Conventional banks request collaterals, charge penalties or re-price the loan facility in case of payment disturbances, and call for guarantees. To the contrary, Islamic banks, being based on principles of *Shari'ah* law, were originally neither allowed to request collaterals nor to re-price contracts (charge penalties), except in the case of a deliberate distortion of payments. As a result, such a contract design was typically associated with moral hazard, which prompted *Shari'ah* scholars to approve charging penalties and requesting collaterals as a method to deter late payment and minimises credit risk (specifically resulting from moral hazard and asymmetric information; Haron and Hock 2007). Such collaterals take the form of *al-rahn*, defined as an asset that secures a deferred obligation that can take the form of cash, gold or silver, shares in equities, or any form of tangible assets or commodities (Iqbal and Mirakhor 2007). Nevertheless, the proceeds resulting from collaterals or levied penalties should only cover the expenses incurred by the bank as a result of default or delay in payments; any additional amounts should be given to a designated charity (Ariffin *et al.* 2009). Approving collaterals and penalties on the one hand mitigates credit risk, and on the other decreases recovery values. Likewise, even though rarely used by Islamic banks, guarantees serve to mitigate credit risk, where the guarantee has to be provided by a third party according to Islamic principles (Ahmed and Khan 2007).

Elgari (2003) suggests that Islamic banks can also manage credit risk by designing two payment schedules: one based on the assumption that the customer will default or delay payments and the other based on regular timely payments, where the mark-up is calculated on the former schedule. Upon completion of the contract, the customer is provided with a refund if they committed to regular payments as described in the second schedule. On a different note, Wilson (2009) demonstrates the importance and usability of non-financial penalties as an effective tool for managing payment defaults in Islamic banks. The inability of defaulters to get refinancing from any other bank after being blacklisted, and the confiscation of assets which act as collateral, seized in case of a default, are two examples of non-financial penalties. Seizing collaterals is only considered as a last resort by the bank because in most cases the asset, a piece of equipment for instance, would be tailored to the client's requirements and thus not be easily sold on.

In addition, a number of credit derivative instruments are heavily used by banks as risk transfer methods, such as Credit Default Swaps (CDS), Asset Backed Securities (ABS) and Collateralised Debt Obligations (CDOs). CDS specifically transfer default risk and are the most common instrument, whereas other traditional instruments like ABS and CDOs are also used to securitise a bundle of homogeneous and heterogeneous instruments, respectively. Hedging credit risk through securitisation requires a well-developed risk management system as well as transparency regarding the involved risk positions to avoid market disturbances (DeutscheBank 2004). However, Islamic banks do not engage in such instruments to hedge credit risk, as the sale of debt, the principle upon which credit derivatives are based, is prohibited by *Shari'ah* law.

With regard to market risks, conventional banks manage to easily transfer such risks by engaging in the derivatives market, for instance, by entering a swap contract to hedge foreign exchange exposures (Meyer 2000). Foreign exchange risk is also managed by setting trading position limits according to the bank's risk tolerance (Santomero 1997). Other contracts are made available, such as options, forwards and futures contracts, to hedge the different components of market risk. However, engaging in the derivatives market and using hedging tools for market risk is prohibited in principle in Islamic banks. Recently, some attempts have been made to create Islamic derivatives instruments, yet such attempts have not yet been approved by the different *Shari'ah* schools and are still under investigation.

Banks face a liquidity problem when expected and unexpected losses occur or in the event of market crises. Such a problem could be severe and might affect the entire banking sector leading to a systemic risk. Hence, banks are requested by the regulatory authorities to perform simulation analysis to investigate their ability for internal financing in the event of crisis and to develop liquidity risk contingency plans (BCBS 2006a). In times when internal financing is not available, banks can access the capital market for the required funds. However, the main challenge faced by conventional banks is when raising funds (liquidity) through capital markets becomes problematic during a time of crisis (Santomero 1997: 20–1). In general, conventional banks hedge risks when liquid markets are available, and internally manage the risks that have no liquid markets by holding assets against untradeable risks (Cumming and Hirtle 2001).

In respect to liquidity risk management in Islamic banks, which represents a major challenge as a result of the lack of *Shari'ah*-compliant liquidity management tools, an institutional framework was recently established to address this problem. This framework comprises the International Islamic Financial Market (IIFM), the Liquidity Management Center (LMC), the Islamic Interbank Money Market (IIMM; introduced by Bank Negara Malaysia) and the Islamic Interbank Cheque Clearing System (IICS; Iqbal and Mirakhor 2007). These institutions mainly aim at providing liquidity management solutions tailored to Islamic financial institutions through standardised products. As yet, these developments have not been fully adopted by the whole Islamic banking market to analyse their performance. More promotion in this regard is required.

As mentioned before, a certain level of capital is required to maintain stability in financial markets; banks with relatively risky assets should hold a higher level of capital than those with less risky assets. However, high levels of capital negatively affect a bank's liquidity, since it reduces deposits and constrains the bank's ability to provide funds. Accordingly, a bank's capital should be kept at a level that ensures profitability as well as stability. Islamic banks are not an exception to this and should manage their capital requirements and use their capital resources efficiently. To reach such a goal, capital resources should be fully identified by maintaining adequate information collection and skills within the bank. Hence, it is necessary for Islamic banks to strengthen their risk management practices to attain a proper definition of their capital requirements; it is acknowledged that the better the risk management employed, the better the ability of the bank to calibrate its capital needs (Grais and Kulathunga 2007). RAROC can be used in Islamic banks to allocate capital to the different modes of financing based on their risk profile. The expected and maximum losses vary from one financing mode to another, and thus can be estimated through the accumulation of historical data. Additionally, it is suggested that RAROC can be used to determine the rate of return on different instruments *ex ante* (Ahmed and Khan 2007).

The profit equalisation reserve (PER) and investment risk reserve (IRR) are risk mitigation tools against *mudaraba* risk attributable to deposit holders. PER is deducted proportionately, between IAHs and shareholders, from the gross income before the bank takes the *mudarib* (fund manager) fees. This reserve ratio is designed to eliminate the variability of profit payouts and maintain a certain level of return to depositors. Similarly, IRR redistributes income over time to cover further losses incurred on investments made with the depositors' funds, as covering such losses with the PER would not comply with *Shari'ah*. It should be noted that restricted account holders face a limited risk to the specified asset/s to which the investment account returns are linked. Furthermore, a clear disclosure and transparency of policies and procedures regarding PER and IRR profit smoothing strategies should be promoted (Sundararajan 2007). In general, Fiennes (2007) suggests that the best protection for IAHs is full disclosure on the bank's side regarding financial results and any major events that would affect the bank's financial position, as well as transparency of contracts and performance measures.

However, limited disclosure of PER, despite being a hedging tool against future losses, may impose risks driven by the uneasiness of IAHs regarding future outcomes. For instance, IAHs may lose trust in a bank's distribution policy and thus withdraw their investments or avoid making further deposits. Moreover, using PER to smooth out today's profits for the sake of future adverse events may be a disadvantage for short-term deposit holders. Accordingly, Greuning and Iqbal (2007) suggest that Islamic banks standardise their treatment of such reserves and consider applying such deductions to long-term depositors only, since short-term depositors are not exposed to long-term risks. Yet, it should be noted that longer-term investors would expect higher returns to compensate their higher exposure to risks and not higher deductions to smooth future returns. Instead, there should be transparency and the appropriate disclosure of accounting treatments to depositors before engagement in a contract to minimise withdrawal risks.

As Islamic banks hold different types of financing contracts, where each contract has a different mix of risks as explained earlier, each contract involves specific mitigation methods that are commonly practised by Islamic banks to minimise the inherent risks. The following section demonstrates the risk mitigation elements embedded in each contract as stipulated by the AAOIFI *Shari'ah* and accounting standards.

5.2 Mitigating risks in contracts

The mitigation methods presented in this section are derived from the AAOIFI accounting and *Shari'ah* standards (2008a, 2008b). Within the requirements specified for each contract, the AAOIFI presents mitigation methods that can be used to manage the different risks per contract. As such, for the risks identified in section 3.3, mitigation tools are presented for a comprehensive risk management process. In general, the mitigation methods presented below are specifically of relevance to credit and operational risks. Other risks, such as market risks, may be mitigated at the overall business level.

In a *murabaha* contract, it has been agreed that the bank may ask the client to pay *hamish jiddiyyah* (a security deposit) before proceeding to buy the requested asset/good. This payment is considered as a down payment requested by the bank to make sure that the client will fulfil his promise in purchasing the ordered good/asset (AAOIFI 2008a). This mitigates the bank's credit risk, specifically in being left with the goods purchased on behalf of the client, as it minimises the risk that the client may refuse to conclude the *murabaha* transaction. Additionally, it is permissible to add into the contract that the bank is not responsible for all or some of the defects of the asset/goods and instead provide the customer with the right to refer back to the supplier for compensation for any defects that are established (AAOIFI 2008b).

Ideally, the full transfer of the ownership of the asset/ goods should be postponed until all instalments are paid. However, banks may include statements in the contract in order to mitigate credit risk. For instance, it may be added within the contract that the bank is entitled to sell the asset/ goods to a third party, on behalf of the customer and on his account, if the customer refuses to take delivery of the specified asset at the determined time. Moreover, despite the fact that Islamic banks are not allowed to impose penalties for delayed payments, they may request guarantees such as cheques or promissory notes to secure the deferred payments upon execution of the *murabaha* contract. Furthermore, it is permitted to charge penalties if the customer deliberately delays in fulfilling the instalments, based on the condition that any amounts received by the bank from such penalties should only be used for charitable purposes. However, this last method of mitigation requires valid proof that the customer deliberately delayed due payments, which should be adequately monitored by the *Shari'ah* board to avoid breach of Islamic principles (AAOIFI 2008b). Similarly, charging penalties, which would eventually be directed towards charitable purposes, may be implemented for the different modes of financing in an Islamic bank.

Relevant to credit risk management, the *Shari'ah* expert Al-Beltagy (for the AAOIFI) added that in practice *murabaha* contracts could be mitigated by what is known as *kafaly al darak*, in which a client recommends a certain supplier based on the latter's experience. In this case, the client guarantees the supplier and not the assets or commodities. As regards to operational risk management, represented in physical capital risk of the *murabaha* contract (identified as ORC01 in the risk coding matrix), the asset or goods subject to the contract should be insured to mitigate possible damage. Insurance for underlying assets is a general mitigation strategy that should be implemented for the different contracts to alleviate the risk of damage of the assets or commodities when under the bank's ownership, until the ownership is transferred to the customer.

To manage delays in payments (credit risk) in an *ijara* or rental contract, the bank may stipulate that the contract would be terminated if the lessee does not pay the rent or fails to pay it on time. Moreover, for the same mitigation purpose, an advance payment of the rental may be taken in respect of the lease upon execution of the contract. The bank may retain this amount were the contract not executed for a reason attributable to the lessee. Similarly, to avoid an early termination of the contract on the side of the customer, the bank could request an initial payment from the customer as a guarantee of the customer's commitment to the lease agreement and the subsequent obligations (AAOIFI 2008b).

Unlike sale contracts, an *ijara* contract has a special feature that allows for setting a floating market rate when pricing the contract. This mitigates market mark-up risk (MRM02), which in this case appears only when identifying rental payments based on fixed rates. In addition, *ijara* contracts may be further utilised in developing mitigation tools, for instance to manage liquidity, since they can be easily securitised: the lessor is allowed to transfer the title, rights and obligations of the leased asset to a third party through a sale contract. This is one major feature that differentiates a sale contract from an *ijara* contract.

The market risk in a *salam* contract, being a product-deferred sale agreement, is high and thus banks usually manage this risk by entering a parallel *salam*. Similarly, operational risk is also high in this type of contract; hence, contracting parties should agree on the terms of settlement in case the delivered goods do not meet the required specifications, where the goods may be accepted at a discounted price, for instance. Furthermore, the subject matter may be secured by a guarantee to minimise settlement (credit) risk (CRX03; AAOIFI 2008b). Finally, an adequate management of the first *salam* contract minimises the possible risks arising as a result of operational aspects within the first *salam* contract.

Similar to the *salam* contract, an *istisna'a* contract is a deferred-sale product that involves high market risk and, hence, a parallel *Istisna'a* contract is usually set up. However, despite having similar features to *salam* contracts, *istisna'a* contracts usually have longer maturities and thus are viewed as having higher risks than *salam* contracts. Consequently, the mitigation methods would vary slightly from those proposed for a *salam* agreement.

For managing credit risk, the purchasing party has the right to request collateral from the manufacturer to guarantee the total amount paid and/or the delivery of assets/ goods in accordance with the pre-agreed time period and specifications. On the other hand, the manufacturer is entitled to obtain collateral that guarantees deferred payments (AAOIFI 2008a). Likewise, it is permissible to give or demand *urboun* (down payment), which is a guarantee in case the contract is rescinded, but which will be considered part of the price if the contract is fulfilled. Such guarantees could be in the form of personal guarantees, current accounts or consent to blocking withdrawal from an account. Moreover, inclusion of a penalty clause is allowed to compensate the purchaser if the manufacturer delays in delivering the subject matter (AAOIFI 2008a).

To mitigate credit risk, specifically in parallel *istisna'a* contracts, it is permissible to state in the contract that the bank is entitled to sell the manufactured/constructed good/asset on behalf of the purchaser if the latter delayed in accepting delivery and/or payment for a certain period of time. In this case, any additional amounts resulting from the sale and exceeding the originally agreed-upon contract price, plus any expenses incurred in the transaction, shall be returned to the original purchaser. On the other hand, if the selling price is lower than the agreed upon contract price, then the bank is entitled to recover the difference from the purchaser (AAOIFI 2008b).

As a method to manage physical capital (operational) risk (ORC04), the parties involved in an *istisna'a* contract should identify a certain period during which the manufacturer or contractor will be liable for any defects that might arise in their work. In addition, the price of the contract may be amended in cases of *force majeure*. Nevertheless, allowing an increase in the amounts to be paid in consideration of an extension of the period of payment should be strictly avoided; this would be considered *riba* and would render the contract invalid. Moreover, since the contract is not binding, the bank has the option to replace the contractor/manufacturer and put in place a new contract to complete the project, but only after undertaking a complete assessment and valuation of the work already done under the first *istisna'a* contract. Another method to manage operational risk is to appoint – with the agreement of all parties – a technically experienced consultant to provide an opinion as to whether the asset/goods under the agreement conform to the agreed-upon contractual specifications (AAOIFI 2008b).

An Islamic bank engaging in a *mudaraba* contract as a financing tool may mitigate the inherent credit risk through requesting appropriate guarantees from the *mudarib*, provided that such guarantees are only utilised by the bank in cases of misconduct or breach of the contract agreement. As indicated by Al-Beltagy (AAOIFI 2008b), collaterals are only allowed in PLS instruments to mitigate moral hazard and not for hedging loss resulting from market or operational events. Additionally, a profit-sharing ceiling may be specified in the contract: parties may agree that if the recognised profit is above a certain amount then additional profits will be attributable to one of the parties, otherwise profit is to be distributed in accordance to the agreed-upon percentage distribution (AAOIFI 2008b).

Other risks involved in a *mudaraba* contract require the bank to undergo prudent assessment for selecting projects before and after providing financing. Part of the assessment may result in the capital provider, in this case the bank, placing restrictions on some actions of the *mudarib* (client), such as restricting the length of the contract or restricting operations to within a certain sector, which could minimise the risk. As a result, Islamic banks usually try to steer away from providing *mudaraba*-based financing tools as they are high risk and mitigation tools are limited.

However, *mudaraba* contracts provided as deposits expose the bank to lower risks, as a result of the profit-and-loss sharing feature embedded within them, despite the other risks that result from this type of contract as elaborated earlier. Possible mitigation methods for these risks are presented in the following section, as part of the overall mitigation methods. However, it is worth noting that, according to the AAOIFI standards (2008b), *mudaraba* losses should be covered from previously earned undistributed profits. Similarly, current losses may be compensated by periodic profits realised in future operations of the *mudaraba* (i.e. future profits may account for past losses).

Here, possible mitigation methods per contract have

been presented based on the AAOIFI standards. Basically, mitigation methods provided within the contract revolve around credit risk. Other risks, such as market risk, are not commonly provided with mitigation methods at contract level but are usually managed at the overall business level, as presented below. Also, Islamic banks should perform an adequate assessment of the value of the underlying assets of all contracts on regular terms (i.e. before, during and after the course of the financing period), to facilitate the identification of appropriate provisions to account for the expected risks.

After elaborating on the common risk mitigation strategies adopted in Islamic banks at both the overall and contract level, it should be noted that financial innovation has opened the door to a constantly developing set of methods for financial institutions to better manage their risks. Yet, when financial innovation is adopted without a full understanding of the underlying structure and principle, it imposes other complex risk exposures. This emphasises the importance of fully understanding the fundamentals and principles of sophisticated risk management techniques and mitigation strategies before embedding them into the risk management process of a bank (Meyer 2000).

5.3 Other risk mitigation methods

Risk transfer strategy, which is also referred to as hedging, is classified under passive risk mitigation strategies. Traditional risk transfer tools are mainly classified into insurance and financial derivatives, both commonly used to transfer risk in conventional banking situations. The latter type involves credit derivatives, swaps, options and forwards/futures, among others. The nature of conventional derivative instruments in principle does not conform to

Shariʿah; yet, there have been attempts to introduce Islamic derivatives, on a limited scale, into the current financial market. This section briefly explores the attempts that have been made in this regard, yet without discussion of the *Shariʿah* acceptance of such financial innovations. A critical evaluation of such hedging tools is not presented here, but the main available Islamic hedging tools are outlined. Among the introduced Islamic risk-transferring techniques are credit derivatives, swaps and *salam*, as well as commodity futures and options.

A new tool for managing credit risk is credit derivatives: the credit and its underlying risk are separated and sold to potential investors who might make a purchase decision if the default risk is acceptable to their individual risk profiles. This can be done by packaging, securitising and marketing credit risk exposures with a variety of credit risk features (Crouhy *et al.* 2001). In the case of Islamic banks, where sale of debt is prohibited, the use of equivalents of credit derivatives is not allowed (except in Malaysia) and falls under heavy criticism from scholars. However, some studies make a distinction between a fully secured as opposed to an unsecured debt. It is argued that external credit assessment makes the quality of a debt transparent as credit valuation techniques have significantly improved. Also, Islamic debt financing is asset-based and is considered as secured financing. Taking these developments into consideration, restrictions on sale of debt may be reconsidered (Chapra and Khan 2000). Some scholars argue that, although sale of debt is not possible in the conventional way, an alternative method can be used where the owner of a debt can appoint a debt collector.

Another instrument of credit risk management is a swap transaction. One definition of a swap is that it is a transaction where parties agree to exchange sets of cash flows over a period of time in the future (Kolb 1997: 613). By using swaps, both parties are better off, which has created a great demand for these contracts. For Islamic Banks, where again the critical factor is whether they are compatible with *Shari'ah*, there should be no objections to the use of swaps. One commonly used contract is a swap which involves exchanging fixed returns with variable returns. Since fixed-rent and adjustable-rent *sukuk* products have only recently been introduced to the markets, an opportunity exists for further financial engineering in the form of *Shari'ah*-compatible swap arrangements. Gassner (2009) states that a return swap, which allows the exchange of impermissible returns with permissible returns, is a flexible instrument that replicates profit-rate swaps and credit-default swaps. However, this method is criticised by some scholars since the proceeds end up in the impermissible sector (Gassner 2009). Some other swaps that can be used by Islamic banks to mitigate various risks are debt-asset swap, swap of liabilities and deposit swaps.

The potential for using futures contracts as a tool for risk control and risk management is tremendous. The use of these contracts in conventional banks to manage their risks is already widespread. Nevertheless, similar to previously mentioned conventional instruments, contemporary futures contracts, in which both payment and receipt of goods/assets are postponed, are prohibited under Islamic law due to the presence of elements of *gharar* and *riba*. In these contracts, payment for the commodity is postponed to a future date, which is prohibited in traditional *fiqh*, where postponing both payment for and delivery of the object of sale is not allowed. Yet, recently, and by virtue of a number of *fiqh* resolutions, conventions and new research, the scope for futures is widening in Islamic finance. Modified futures contracts are used by Islamic banks taking into consideration *Shari'ah* principles. Some types of forwards and futures that are used by Islamic banks are *salam* and commodity futures as well as currency forwards and futures. For example, Kamali (2005) argues that futures contracts could be reconsidered if new technology is able to eliminate any *gharar* in the contract, so in the future these contracts may be used in managing commodities risk.

In addition, forwards and futures are one of the most effective instruments for hedging against currency risks. Although all scholars unanimously agree about the prohibition of such contracts by *Shari'ah*, most Islamic banks that have significant exposure to foreign exchange risk do use currency forwards and futures for hedging purposes as required by the regulators. It is important to note that the consensus among scholars is that currency futures and forwards are another form of *riba*, which is prohibited by *Shari'ah*. Keeping this apparent contradiction in view and the tremendous difference between the stability of the present and past markets, Chapra and Khan (2000) make a suggestion to *Shari'ah* scholars to review their position and allow Islamic banks to use these contracts for hedging. It may be noted that hedging is not an income-earning activity, and since *riba* is a source of income, there is no question of the involvement of *riba*. Moreover, they argue that hedging actually reduces *gharar* and thus should be encouraged. By taking up this suggestion, any contradiction between *fiqh* positions and actual bank practices should be overcome, empowering Islamic banks with much-needed contracts.

Options are another powerful risk management instrument that is once again prohibited by resolution of the Islamic *Fiqh* Academy. This limits the ability of Islamic banks to use options as a risk management tool at present. However, some other forms of options that can be used under *Shari'ah* are *khyiar al-shart* (option by stipulation), *khyiar al-tayeen* (option of determination or choice), *khyiar al-ayb* (option for defect), *khyiar al-ruyat* (option after inspection) and *khyiar al-majlis* (option of session). The framework underlying *al-khyiar* in general is the equity of the contract and satisfaction of the parties to the contract. Hence, transparency regarding the counter values being exchanged, as well as the consequences of the contract, must be clearly communicated among parties (Obaidullah 2002).[1]

Ghoul (2008a) elaborates that Islamic financial-product development is lagging behind in developing Islamic hedging instruments designed to lower overall risk exposure. Ghoul acknowledges that Islamic derivatives, such as forwards, futures and options contracts, are not broadly accepted by the majority of Islamic scholars since such contracts are zero-sum games in which one party gains at the expense of the other and they do not involve a real transfer of physical assets (are not backed by assets), thus opening the door for speculative activities. Options contracts usually do not involve transfer of the underlying asset, which marks them as impermissible under *Shari'ah*. However, financial markets currently offer some Islamic products, such as *salam* contracts, which are alternatives to futures and forwards. Additionally, *bai-urbun* and *khiyar al-shart* are two alternatives for options contracts, though the former is rarely accepted by the different Islamic schools.

In addition, the role of securitisation in transferring the risk should be emphasised, as it is essential in mitigating liquidity risk. Yet, securitisation and sale of debt remains controversial among *Shari'ah* scholars. Chapra (2007) provides some arguments that support the permissibility of the sale of debt, arguing that it is secured on the basis that it is a sale of an asset-based debt in which a bank is selling part of an asset and the buyer is receiving a share of the profit the bank is gaining on the back of this debt-based transaction (*murabaha* for instance). While the argument remains, securitisation is moving forward in the Islamic finance industry, mainly represented by *sukuk* issuance and backed by different contract types.

Finally, as stated by Gassner (2009), the current nature of the available Islamic hedging tools is just a replication of the available conventional tools. Such a replication is not appropriate for Islamic products, as it does not fit with its underlying *Shari'ah* principles. On the other hand, Gassner suggests that Islamic finance needs hedging tools that are of benefit to the economy not just replicas of conventional finance hedging tools. So, Islamic finance remains in need of innovative mitigation tools that meet its main objectives. Further research is required in this area to develop and to assess the validity of the currently offered hedging tools for Islamic finance.

Having explored the main steps of a risk management process, the importance of applying an integrated risk management framework should be emphasised, whereby risk management applications and procedures for different business units are reported to key decision-makers. Such an integrated system allows the bank to allocate capital efficiently and capture the bank's various risks. Furthermore, a bank's management can easily evaluate the risk management performance by comparing the *ex post* and *ex ante* performance results, in which returns are evaluated with regard to the risks taken.

Iqbal and Mirakhor (2007) recommend that Islamic banks should adopt a robust comprehensive risk management framework, similar to conventional banks, to reduce exposures to risks and enhance their compatibility in the market. To implement such a framework the cooperation of the management of Islamic banks, regulators and supervisors is required. Additionally, this process should take into consideration *Shari'ah* compliance issues. Currently, Islamic financial institutions realise the importance of having a comprehensive risk management framework to help sustain further growth of the industry (Greuning and Iqbal 2007). However, Cumming and Hirtle (2001) summarise two main obstacles that hinder the presence of a consolidated risk management system. First, is the cost of integrating, compiling and analysing information from different business lines/units and, second, is the regulatory cost imposed on the banking business (for example, in the capital and liquidity requirements set by regulators). The next chapter demonstrates how to adapt an integrated risk management framework to fit Islamic banks, by presenting a hypothetical case of an Islamic bank and adopting suggested risk management procedures based on earlier discussions. The adopted risk management application takes into consideration the discussed risk management challenges.

Note

1. For more details about Islamic options, refer to H. Ahmed and T. Khan (2007), 'Risk management in Islamic banking', in M. K. Hassan and K. L. Lewis (eds), *Handbook of Islamic Banking*. Cheltenham: Edward Elgar Publishing.

CHAPTER 6

AN APPLICATION OF RISK MANAGEMENT TO ISLAMIC BANKS

This chapter specifically presents a case study of adopting an integrated approach to manage the inherent risks in Islamic banks. The case study is presented as a conceptual Islamic bank model that was developed based on real data derived from Islamic banks' annual reports. The bank model is used as an example to explain how the integrated risk management framework should be applied in order to address the challenges of risk management currently faced by Islamic banks. The model elaborates on how returns are distributed based on the different classifications of deposit facilities. Moreover, different scenarios are used to show how risks are assessed. Finally, the methods that can be utilised to mitigate the associated risks are suggested.

6.1 The Islamic bank model

Before presenting the case study, the characteristics of Islamic banks are discussed in this section. The theoretical/simulated model has been developed based on the operational model of the largest Islamic banks.[1] It provides a clear classification of the different financing modes to simulate the analysis of risks in Islamic banks. The model presented not only covers the common practices of Islamic banks but also extends to cover other less-common Islamic financing instruments, such as *salam* and *istisna'a*, to extend the risk analysis to such instruments being included on the balance sheet. Furthermore, it takes into account the Profit Equalisation Reserve (PER) and Investment Risk Reserve (IRR) as main concepts in profit distribution, which is not a common disclosure in Islamic banks despite being a required disclosure according to the AAOIFI accounting standards. To avoid discrepancies in financial reporting and *Shari'ah* standards, the bank model is developed in accordance with the accounting and *Shari'ah* standards issued by the AAOIFI (see AAOIFI 2008a, 2008b). The main financial statements presented include the balance sheet, income statement and the distribution of profits among different stakeholders.[2]

The bank model follows the accounting and *Shari'ah* standards issued by the AAOIFI, as explained above. Furthermore, the model assumes homogenous products and portfolios to simplify the quantification process; in fact it is believed that Islamic banks' business models and products are homogenous in an attempt to reduce the risk arising from product arrangements (Heiko and Cihak 2008). Also, the model does not present a segmented analysis (i.e. it does not analyse the different banking activities in terms of treasury, retail, corporate or investment banking). To simplify the model it focuses on the main Islamic banking activities divided into the possible operating modes, as explained in earlier chapters, and excludes trading activities (i.e. securities, commodities or equities).

The structure of the balance sheet is critically important for the risk management process, since an analytical view of a bank's balance sheet components helps to determine the level of the risks faced by the bank, such as liquidity, market and credit risks. A change in the structure of the bank's balance sheet causes a change in the underlying risks. This indicates that risk management policies and procedures should not be implemented without first analysing the balance sheet. It is worth noting that although the components of Islamic banks' balance sheet are almost identical, the proportionate weights vary enormously among the different banks worldwide (Greuning and Iqbal 2008), which affects the relevant risk profiles.

The asset side of the balance sheet constitutes liquid, financing, investment, fixed and other assets. Liquid assets are mainly represented by cash balances and equivalents, and commodity *murabaha*, where commodity *murabaha* (also referred to as *tawarruq*) is a short-term instrument used to manage liquidity within Islamic banks at low profits. Theoretically, it is defined as the purchase of a commodity from one party on credit for the purpose of immediate sale to another party for cash, thus providing liquidity. In practice, it is usually conducted through the London Metal Exchange (LME): the bank purchases a commodity from the market, sells it back to the customer for a deferred payment, and the bank sells it on the LME for cash on behalf of the customer, being the customer's agent[3] (Abozaid 2010). *Tawarruq* or commodity *murabaha* is widely practised by Islamic banks (Dusuki 2010). For example, if an Islamic bank has an excess liquidity of USD 10 million, it can invest this amount through another bank, where the investing bank receives a commission for investing this amount in a *Shari'ah*-compliant investment or an Islamic financing activity. Financing assets are represented as receivable amounts in the different financing modes, namely, *mudaraba, murabaha, ijara, istisna'a* and *salam*. *Musharaka* financing is excluded from the presented model since it closely resembles *mudaraba* (though is slightly less

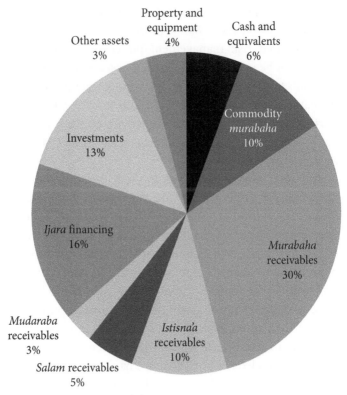

Figure 6.1 *Composition of assets*

risky). Hence, the risk analysis to be applied to *musharaka* will be similar to that of *mudaraba*. As for investments and other assets, they represent long-term investments that can be further classified into available-for-sale, reported as fair-value reserves or held-to-maturity investments. Finally, fixed assets include the bank's infrastructure, such as computer equipment, furniture, land, and all premises from which the bank operates. Figure 6.1 elaborates on the composition of the assets within the presented model.

Within the Islamic bank model presented here the

liabilities consist of those due to financial institutions, customers' accounts (deposits) and other liabilities. The amounts due to financial institutions represent deposits extended between banks. Customers' accounts can be current accounts or Profit-Sharing Investment Accounts (PSIA). The former type are customers' deposits that are regarded as safekeeping deposits that bear no return, sometimes referred to as *qard hassan*. Rosly and Zaini (2008) explain that Islamic banks provide such services/facilities to fulfil their clients transactional needs, where the principal amount is guaranteed with no returns provided. Profits arising from such accounts are attributable to the bank's equity since the bank guarantees the principal amounts of such accounts. Current accounts in this case are based on the *Shari'ah* rule *al-kharaj bel daman*, which means that if a principal amount is guaranteed, then profits and losses are attributable to the guarantor.

On the other hand, PSIA are provided as long-term instruments based on a *mudaraba* agreement between the bank and its clients. PSIA can either be saving investment accounts or fixed investment accounts (F-PSIA). Saving investment accounts have no defined maturities, sometimes referred to as open access accounts, from which clients may withdraw the deposited amounts at any point in time. However, fixed investment accounts have defined maturities: customers agree not to withdraw the deposited amounts before the agreed upon maturity date. Within the model, the employed maturities are three, six and twelve months, while F-PSIA, which have contract lengths of more than one year, are referred to as open-maturity F-PSIA (see Figure 6.2). This classification of customers' accounts has important implications for the risk analysis, which will be provided within the risk analysis section. Other liabilities include the unpaid depositors' share of profits, such as the

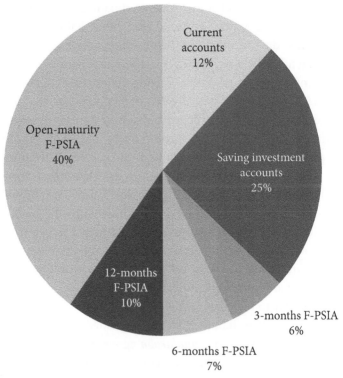

Figure 6.2 *Distribution of depositors' accounts*

deducted amounts attributable to depositors' PER from previous years, as well as other sundry items. Deferred profit is neither recognised as a liability nor an equity by the AAOIFI (AAOIFI 2008a: 193–200), hence it is placed in between the liabilities and equities. Finally, total equity is divided into share capital, reserves and retained earnings (see Table 6.1).

As presented in Table 6.2, the income statement constitutes the operating income represented by the contributions of each of the financing, investment and services activities (as shown in Figure 6.3), the operating expenditures, as well as the deductions attributable to the PER and IRR before

Table 6.1 *Islamic bank balance sheet (in USD)*

Balance sheet at 31 December 2008

Assets		Liabilities and equity	
		Due to financial institutions	2,500,000
Cash and equivalents	6,000,000	Current accounts	7,560,000
Commodity *murabaha*	10,000,000	Saving investment accounts	15,750,000
Murabaha Receivables	30,000,000	3-months F-PSIA	3,780,000
Istisna'a receivables	10,000,000	6-months F-PSIA	4,410,000
Salam receivables	5,000,000	12-months F-PSIA	6,300,000
Mudaraba receivables	3,000,000	Open-maturity F-PSIA	25,200,000
Total receivables other than *ijara*	**58,000,000**	**Total depositors' accounts**	**63,000,000**
		Other liabilities	1,150,000
Ijara financing	16,000,000	Profit for the year	7,350,000
		Total liabilities	66,650,000
Investments	13,000,000	Deferred profit	12,000,000
Other assets	3,000,000	**Shareholders' equity**	
Property and equipment	4,000,000	Share capital	9,000,000
		Reserves	3,000,000
		Retained earnings	2,000,000
		Total equity	**14,000,000**
Total assets	**100,000,000**	**Total equity and liabilities**	**100,000,000**

Table 6.2 *Islamic bank income statement (in USD)*

Income statement year end 2008	
Financing income	8,400,000
Investment income	2,040,000
Fees, commissions and foreign exchange income	1,080,000
Other income	480,000
Total operating income	**12,000,000**
Employees' costs	−1,250,000
G&A expenses	−750,000
Depreciation	−500,000
Provisions for impairment	−2,150,000
Total operating expenditure	**−4,650,000**
Net profit before PER, IRR and distributions to IAHs	**7,350,000**
PER	−735,000
Net profit after PER	**6,615,000**
Mudarib fees	904,530
Profit after *mudarib* fees	**3,618,118**
IRR	−180,906
Distributions to IAHs	−3,437,212
Net profit before taxes and *zakah*	**2,996,882**

distributions to PSIA holders. Financing income originates from sale-based and PLS financing activities practised by the bank, while investment income comprises income received from the investment assets acquired by the bank, such as investments in properties and/or associates. Fees, commissions and foreign exchange income include fee-based income received from services provided by the bank, such as fund management and financial advisory services. Other income may include, among others, gains (losses) on asset revaluation as well as other sundry non-bank related income. With regard to the operating expenditures, the significant item is provisions for impairment, which are the amounts related specifically to credit risk associated with

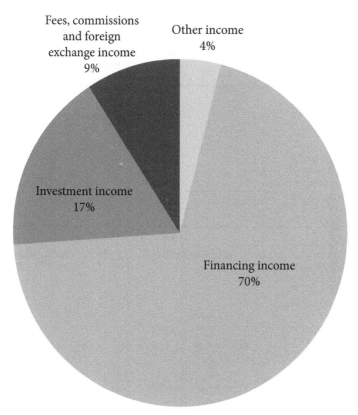

Figure 6.3 *Profit contributions*

financing and investment activities. Hence, the provisions for impairment are critical to the analysis of credit risk. Finally, PER and IRR are deducted before any distributions are made to PSIA holders.

To illustrate profit distributions and invested amounts in the different depositors' accounts, Table 6.3 is provided. As illustrated in the Islamic bank income statement, the bank first deducts the operating expenditure from the operating income before any further deductions or distributions

Table 6.3 *Profit distributions schedule (in USD)*

	Invested % from principal amounts	Average balances	Invested amounts	% Distributions of profits	Allocated profit	PER (10%)
Depositors' investment accounts						
Saving investment accounts	60	15,750,000	9,450,000	15.0	1,101,205	110,120
3-months F-PSIA	70	3,780,000	2,646,000	4.2	308,337	30,834
6-months F-PSIA	75	4,410,000	3,307,500	5.2	385,422	38,542
12-months F-PSIA	80	6,300,000	5,040,000	8.0	587,309	58,731
Open-maturity F-PSIA	90	25,200,000	22,680,000	36.0	2,642,891	264,289
Total depositors' (IAHs) investments		55,440,000	43,123,500	68.4	5,025,164	502,516
Shareholders' investments						
Capital	100	9,000,000	9,000,000	14.3	1,048,766	104,877
Reserves	100	3,000,000	3,000,000	4.8	349,589	34,959
Current accounts and equivalents	40	19,876,500	7,950,600	12.6	926,480	92,648
Mudarib fees						
Total shareholders' equity		31,876,500	19,950,600	31.6	2,324,836	232,484

[a] Investment returns distributed to depositors (IAHs) are calculated by dividing profit after IRR by the relevant average balances. Similarly, the returns attributable to shareholders' equity are accounted for as a percentage of the average balance of the total shareholders' equity.

take place. Distributions to PSIA holders (saving and fixed deposit account holders) are based on the share of their invested amounts in the deposited principals, hence, as an initial step, the bank calculates the invested amounts from the different sources of funds, based on the bank's policy towards assigning the appropriate percentages to be invested from each source of fund. For instance, in the model presented, 60 per cent of the saving investment

	Profit after PER	*Mudarib* fees (20%)	Profit after *mudarib* fees	IRR (5%)	Profit after IRR	Investment returns[a] (%)
Depositors' investment accounts						
Saving investment accounts	991,084	198,217	792,867	39,643	753,224	4.78
3-months F-PSIA	277,504	55,501	222,003	11,100	210,903	5.58
6-months F-PSIA	346,880	69,376	277,504	13,875	263,628	5.98
12-months F-PSIA	528,578	105,716	422,863	21,143	401,720	6.38
Open-maturity F-PSIA	2,378,602	475,720	1,902,882	95,144	1,807,738	7.17
Total depositors' (IAHs) investments	**4,522,648**	**904,530**	**3,618,118**	**180,906**	**3,437,212**	**6.20**
Shareholders' investments						
Capital	943,890		943,890		943,890	
Reserves	314,630		314,630		314,630	
Current accounts and equivalents	833,832		833,832		833,832	
Mudarib fees			904,530		904,530	
Total shareholders' equity	**2,092,352**		**2,996,882**		**2,996,882**	**24.97**

accounts are utilised by the bank for financing investments, whereas the percentages assigned to PSIAs range between 70 and 90 per cent. The amounts that are left uninvested are allocated to the current accounts and equivalents from which 40 per cent in total are used in financing and investment activities by the bank (see Table 6.3). On the other hand, 100 per cent of the bank's equity is used to finance the bank's activities. After determining the invested amounts from each source of fund, for example, USD 9,450,000 for saving investment accounts, the percentage of profit distributions can be calculated by dividing the invested amount by the total investments allocated by the bank, so 15 per cent (9,450,000/{43,123,500+19,950,600}) represents the share of profits allocated to investment accounts. Afterwards, the PER is deducted from both PSIA holders and shareholders; within the presented bank model, 10 per cent is deducted from each. Further deductions of *mudarib* fees (20%) and IRR (5%) are applied only to PSIA holders, based on the AAOIFI accounting standards. Finally, it should be noted that PER relating to shareholders is added to the shareholders equity, while PER and IRR attributable to IAHs are included with the liabilities of the bank.

Such an aggregation of profit distribution is deemed necessary for risk management. It requires clear presentation that differentiates between depositors' (IAHs) accounts, which will be utilised in the following sections. The explained profit distribution is a general stipulation of the AAOIFI accounting standards (AAOIFI 2008a: 197–204). The AAOIFI standards state that profits should be allocated proportionally between the bank and IAHs on the basis of the amounts of funds contributed by each party (as presented within the bank model), or may be distributed on the basis of agreed-upon percentages between parties. It is worth noting that some Islamic banks only share profits that arise from certain activities, such as financing and investment activities, while entirely retaining returns that arise from any other source of income, such as commissions income or trading income. On the other hand, if the bank incurs losses, then they should first be deducted from undistributed profits. If the losses are not fully covered by this, then the remaining amount should be deducted from the respective equity contributions. Nevertheless, when loss results due to misconduct on the bank's side, it should only be deducted from the Islamic bank's share of the profits (AAOIFI 2008a: 210, 218).

6.2 Risk analysis

On the overall bank level, Islamic banks hold different views regarding the significance of risks, which depend greatly on their operational activities and the market/s in which the bank operates. For instance, Ariffin *et al.* (2009) revealed that Islamic banks perceive credit risk as the most critical risk, followed by liquidity and foreign exchange risks, whereas *Shari'ah* risk is perceived as the least important on an average basis. However, it is argued that in practice credit risk is viewed as the least important among Islamic bank risks, backed by the fact that on the contractual level there are various available methods to mitigate credit risk that do not contradict the ideals of *Shari'ah*. Similarly, an earlier survey conducted by Khan and Ahmed (2001) indicated that credit risk was considered the least severe of Islamic bank risks, whereas mark-up risk was ranked as the most significant risk, followed by operational risk and liquidity risk, respectively. It is important to note here that all the reported views regarding the ranking of risk severity are based on qualitative analysis through conducting surveys, as a result of a lack of data to quantify each risk and compare their severity. Regardless of the perceived severity of the different risks, Islamic banks should undertake a comprehensive analysis of all underlying risks in order to meet the criteria of an integrated risk management approach.

It is worth noting that following the recent banking crisis the Bank for International Settlements (BIS) emphasised the importance of risk concentrations, defined as 'any single exposure or group of similar exposures with the potential to produce (i) losses large enough to threaten a bank's credit worthiness or ability to maintain its core operations or (ii) a material change in a bank's risk profile' (BCBS 2009: 16).

Risk concentrations may arise as a result of exposure to a single counterparty, specific industry or economic sector, or geographical region, or from credit risk mitigation techniques, such as being exposed to similar collaterals (BCBS 2009). Hence, similar to conventional banks, Islamic banks should integrate risk concentrations within the overall analysis (identification and assessment) of risk exposures. Such integration can be achieved through building up scenario analysis, which considers common or correlated risk factors that reflect concentrations among risks under both normal and stressed market conditions. Greuning and Iqbal (2008) concede that Islamic banks lack diversification in their deposits and assets base, meaning that the benefits that arise from geographic and product diversification have yet to be fully explored. Greuning and Iqbal also perceive that Islamic banks could reduce their exposure to displaced commercial and withdrawal risks by diversifying their depositor base.

Considering the current status and relative newness of the Islamic banking industry, determining the correlation among different risk factors represents a major challenge to the industry because, as yet, Islamic banks lack supporting data inputs. This challenge can only be met through a vigorous application of a fully integrated risk management framework that involves adequate reporting and identification of risks. In due course, this framework will provide a database with the required set of inputs to facilitate risk analysis and incorporate correlation events.

Identified credit risks on the individual level should be accumulated and assessed on a portfolio basis to determine the degree of overall credit risk that the bank holds on its balance sheet. Moreover, a lack of diversification among different portfolios, counterparties, financing facilities and markets increases the overall credit risk. Assignment of assets based on their risk profile can only be achieved by conducting individual risk analysis for each financing instrument, as the first step towards risk identification. Further diversification analysis may be provided for each portfolio by analysing the involved counterparties and markets. In general, diversification has a positive effect towards credit risk management as it reduces correlation among risk events.

Examining the balance sheets of a sample of Islamic banks, the largest by total assets revealed low contributions to risky assets such as *salam* and high contributions to less risky assets such as *murabaha*. Specifically, the sample showed contributions of 69, 13, 4, 7 and 5 per cent of total financing activities for *murabaha, ijara, istisna'a, mudaraba* and *musharaka*, respectively, with no disclosures of *salam* financing in any of the sample banks except for Al-Baraka bank, which disclosed 2 per cent *salam* financing of the total financing activities. Hence, it is clear that Islamic banks concentrate their financing activities within *murabaha*, which is recognised as the product with the lowest risk. However, the presented conceptual Islamic bank model provides a more diverse portfolio of assets that consists of five financing facilities, namely *murabaha, istisna'a, salam, mudaraba* and *ijara*, representing 30, 10, 5, 3 and 16 per cent of total assets, respectively.

On the overall bank level, the market value of conventional banks is clearly affected by fluctuations in interest rates. However, the market value of Islamic banks, theoretically, should not be sensitive to interest rate fluctuations since their activities are not based on interest rates. Nevertheless, as Islamic banks operate in dual financial systems, the market value of the overall bank is indirectly affected by interest rate fluctuations. This is empirically tested by Chattha and Bacha (2010), who contend that Islamic banks are more vulnerable to interest rate risks by examining their duration gaps relative to peer conventional banks. The examined sample demonstrated that Islamic banks have higher duration mismatches between assets and liabilities, which imply higher exposures to interest rate risk. On average, the Islamic banks' assets showed longer maturities and were more of a fixed-rate nature (not subject to re-pricing) compared to conventional banks' assets, though both banking groups revealed almost the same maturities on the deposits side. The fixed-rate nature of the assets side can be explained by the assets side being dominated by *murabaha* contracts in which the price is predetermined and not subject to change. Another important aspect that contributes to the overall market risk is the lack of diversification in the client base, the different markets (international and domestic) or the various sectors. The importance of diversification was made clear during the recent sub-prime crisis in the Gulf area, which was indirectly affected by the decline in real estate prices as banks were highly exposed to the real estate sector through investments. This is clearly seen in the annual reports.[4]

From the above, it can be inferred that the main overall market risk factors, ignoring foreign exchange risk for simplicity, are market interest-rate fluctuations, diversification and maturity of assets and deposits. Consequently, the diversification policy and balance-sheet maturity structure greatly affect the market risk of an Islamic bank, whereas interest rate fluctuations remain an external factor that affects its total market value. The diversification policy should reflect the bank's strategy towards various market conditions and future expectations. The maturity structure of an Islamic bank's balance sheet is affected by three elements: the maturity structure of assets, the allocated amounts for investments from the different types of deposits (Table 6.4) and the maturity structure of the invested

Table 6.4 *Allocation of investments from different investment accounts (in USD)*

	Average balances	Basis for investment	Invested amounts	Uninvested amounts
Depositors' investment accounts				
Saving investment accounts	15,750,000	60%	9,450,000	6,300,000
Fixed deposits investment accounts 3 m	3,780,000	70%	2,646,000	1,134,000
Fixed deposits investment accounts 6 m	4,410,000	75%	3,307,500	1,102,500
Fixed deposits investment accounts 12 m	6,300,000	80%	5,040,000	1,260,000
Fixed deposits investment accounts open	25,200,000	90%	22,680,000	2,520,000
Total depositors' investment	**55,440,000**		**43,123,500**	**12,316,500**
Shareholders' investment				
Capital	9,000	100%	9,000,000	—
Reserves	3,000,000	100%	3,000,000	—
Current accounts	7,560,000	40%	3,024,000	4,536,000
Depositors' un-invested amounts	12,316,500	40%	4,926,600	7,389,900
Total shareholders' investment	**31,876,500**		**19,950,600**	**11,925,900**

Table 6.5 *Maturity structure of invested amounts*

Maturity structure of invested amounts			
	Less than 1 year	From 1 to 5 years	More than 5 years	Total
Current accounts and equivalent	40%	60%	0%	100%
Saving investment accounts	20%	45%	35%	100%
Time deposits	10%	35%	55%	100%
Capital and reserves	0%	0%	100%	100%

amounts (Table 6.5), where the last two elements mainly impact the maturity structure of deposits.

To elaborate on the elements that affect the maturity structure of an Islamic bank, consider the presented bank model. The maturity structure is dominated by short- and medium-term assets, contributing 43 per cent of total assets, mainly through engaging in *murabaha* (30%) and *ijara* (16%) financing. With regard to the second element, the allocated amounts from different investment deposits, an Islamic bank allocates only a proportion of the deposited amounts to investment purposes, the incurred returns from which are distributed among the bank and its IAHs (as depicted on p. 141). Within the presented bank model, the bank chooses to invest 60 per cent of saving investment accounts, 70 per cent of fixed deposits accounts with three months maturity, 100 per cent of the capital, 40 per cent of current accounts, and so forth, as shown in Table 6.4. The uninvested amounts may be treated similarly to current accounts, and the bank may choose to allocate larger

Table 6.6 *Maturity structure of the balance sheet*

Maturity structure based on balance sheet structure				
Maturity	Less than 1 year	From 1 to 5 years	More than 5 years	Total
Assets	24,250,000	42,750,000	33,000,000	100,000,000
	24%	43%	33%	100%
Liabilities	20,363,490	23,308,585	42,327,925	
Capital and reserves	0	0	14,000,000	100,000,000
	20%	23%	56%	100%
Maturity gaps	3,886,510	19,441,415	−23,327,925	0

amounts to investments made at its own risk meaning that IAHs neither share in the profits nor losses incurred from such investments.

Finally, after determining the amounts to be invested, their maturity structure should be specified; for example, of the USD 9.5 million invested from the saving accounts, 20 per cent are invested for one year, 45 per cent for a range of one to five years, and 35 per cent for more than five years. Similarly, other available investments are allocated for different maturities, as shown in Table 6.5. As such, the bank's strategy towards allocating certain amounts and specifying the composition of investment deposits to different maturities shapes the final maturity structure of deposits. Table 6.6 provides the resulting maturity structure of the bank's balance sheet, allowing for further risk assessment, for instance through gap or duration analysis. It should also be noted that the maturity mismatches are essential for liquidity risk analysis.

As illustrated previously, liquidity risks in both Islamic and conventional banks are the same by definition. In fact, the sources of liquidity risk in Islamic banks are typical of those of conventional banks; however, the available management tools differ as a result of the *Shari'ah* requirements, which increases the severity of liquidity risk for Islamic banks. The lack of liquidity management tools puts banks under the pressure of holding higher levels of cash and/or liquid assets, which affects their profitability and increases the opportunity cost for Islamic banks. This is a major problem for the industry and needs to be resolved to help Islamic banks move forward. Currently, various attempts are being made to provide liquidity management instruments for the market. The sources of liquidity risk may be classified into indirect and direct sources. Indirect sources arise from any distortions in cash flows caused by market, operational or business risks and resulting in a liquidity problem, either causing a liquid deficit or surplus. Direct sources of risk may result from delays or defaults in due payments, deposit withdrawals, the ability to raise funds (to refinance or to meet obligations) and asset liability maturity mismatch.

Another risk that appears relatively more significant for Islamic banks than their conventional counterparts is operational risk. In general, this is caused by the relatively sophisticated contractual obligations of Islamic banks as most of the offered financing instruments are provided through more than one financial contract, which increases operational risk. In addition, some risks that are specific to Islamic banks are added to operational risk, namely ownership risk and *Shari'ah* risk. Ownership risk is classified as a component of physical capital risk, whereas the risk of *Shari'ah* compliance is embedded within all operational aspects, for which the bank's responsibility as a *mudarib* is the same. Failure to comply with *Shari'ah* greatly jeopardises the reputation of an Islamic bank, leading to reputational risk. For this reason, as explained earlier,

Shari'ah boards are assigned to verify that a bank's various activities are conducted in accordance to *Shari'ah* jurisprudence. However, as Islamic banks operate within a global and highly interactive financial system, existing market forces, such as competition and required international standards, greatly challenge *Shari'ah* compliance issues that in some cases stand as a barrier to a competitive banking business. In terms of market competition, Islamic banks are challenged to provide competitive returns to their IAHs and competitive banking products and services while complying with *Shari'ah*. However, it is well known that the Islamic finance industry has struggled to agree on common principles and interpretations of *Shari'ah* law worldwide, which causes discrepancies in the application and acceptance of financial products (Valente 2009).

Other sources of operational risks are legal risk, systems risk and human risk. Islamic banks should be able to identify legal risk based on the environment in which the bank operates, knowing that *Shari'ah* jurisprudence is not applied in the diverse legal environment. In addition, it is well acknowledged that legal risk may have a substantial impact on Islamic banks, because of the lack of reliable legal systems and the uncertainty in the interpretation of financial contracts, amongst other factors (Sundararajan and Errico 2002; Hassan and Dicle 2005; Izhar 2010). Furthermore, Izhar (2010) adds that financial innovations contribute considerably to legal risk. Model risk, arising from the use of advanced information systems and management tools such as risk control models, should be fully understood, as it may lead to intolerable problems. The human capital of Islamic banks should have both *Shari'ah* and financial knowledge, because any lack of knowledge will increase the likelihood of operational errors. Currently, human risk contributes highly to operational risk because of a lack of adequate personnel, knowledgeable and adequately trained in both areas: *Shari'ah* jurisprudence and financial issues.

Finally, Islamic banks are exposed to similar business risks as conventional banks that arise from different macro-economic, political and systemic conditions. Systemic and political risks are similar for both banking systems, even though it can be inferred that systemic risk will be higher in Islamic banks because of current disclosure practices, transparency and *Shari'ah* rulings. On the other hand, theoretically, Islamic banks will be less vulnerable to market shocks, as they can shift losses to IAHs during such times, using the PLS principle. However, this shift would cause the bank a reputational loss (business risk). Hence, Islamic banks need to be explicitly transparent and clear when disclosing the extent of possible loss exposures attributable to both IAHs and shareholders. Additionally, Islamic banks face business pressures to provide competitive innovative products in a *Shari'ah*-compliant manner. This includes developing short-term liquidity instruments and resource mobilisation at a competitive cost (IFSB 2007: 29).

Although withdrawal risk exists in conventional banks, it is viewed as a more serious risk for Islamic banks (Ahmed 2006), mainly driven by two factors: the returns distributed to IAHs and *Shari'ah* compliance. As stated by Izhar (2010), IAHs in Islamic banks expect competitive returns, not only compared to other Islamic banks but also to their conventional counterparts, and require *Shari'ah* compliance in all aspects of the banking business. Divergence in either of these two areas – rate-of-return risk or *Shari'ah* risk – exposes Islamic banks to withdrawal risk. Market competition forces Islamic banks to provide competitive profit rates to their deposit holders, yet the profit rates earned by most of the Islamic banks' assets are not subject to changes in market rates because the prices of these assets, mainly *murabaha*, are predetermined and based on previous market rates (Iqbal and Molyneux 2005). Therefore, the profit earned by the bank on the assets side highly affects the business of the bank and its position within the market. Rate-of-return risk and withdrawal risk further drive displaced commercial risk, as Islamic banks may sacrifice part of the profits attributable to equity holders for the sake of deposit holders or may transfer losses attributable to deposit holders to equity holders. An Islamic bank will undertake such actions to minimise further business risks, such as withdrawal and/or reputational risks.

6.3 Scenario analysis

Having elaborated on the risk exposures facing Islamic banks on the overall business level, it is now necessary to provide some examples that explain the integration among risks and to demonstrate risk analysis through the application of different scenarios. As regards to risk integration, assume that the presented Islamic bank concentrates its *ijara* financing in real estate in the Gulf area, exposing the bank to credit risk (concentration risk). Following the subprime financial crisis, prices of real estate in the Gulf area witnessed large declines. Thus, the *ijara* portfolio witnessed defaults causing the bank's financing income to drop by 20 per cent, falling to 6.72 million from a previous figure of 8.4 million. Accordingly, the bank increases impairment provisions by 5 per cent to reach 2.26 million instead of 2.15 million, as shown in Table 6.7.

In this scenario, the credit concentration risk to which the bank is exposed triggers rate-of-return risk, withdrawal risk and displaced commercial risk. First, concentration risk leads to a lower distribution of returns to IAHs, as shown in Table 6.8, which in turn exposes the bank to

Table 6.7 *Scenario 1 – effect of concentration risk on the bank's income statement (in USD)*

Income statement year end		
	Base case	Scenario case 1
Financing income	8,400,000	6,720,000
Investment income	2,040,000	2,040,000
Fees, commissions and foreign exchange income	1,080,000	1,080,000
Other income	480,000	480,000
Operating income	**12,000,000**	**10,320,000**
Employees' costs	−1,250,000	−1,250,000
G&A expenses	−750,000	−750,000
Depreciation	−500,000	−500,000
Provisions for impairment	−2,150,000	−2,257,500
Operating expenditures	**−4,650,000**	**−4,757,500**
Net profit before PER, IRR and distributions to IHAs	**7,350,000**	**5,562,500**
PER	−735,000	−556,250
Net profit after PER	**6,615,000**	**5,006,250**
IRR	−180,906	−136,910
Distributions to deposit holders	−3,437,212	−2,601,292
Net profit before taxes and *zakah*	**2,996,882**	**2,268,048**
Average number of shares outstanding	**5,000,000**	**5,000,000**
EPS	**0.599**	**0.454**

rate-of-return risk if other banks in the market offer higher returns to their depositors. Hence, eventually the bank is exposed to withdrawal risk as depositors would be expected to withdraw their investments from the bank and move them elsewhere. In this case the bank is expected to respond

Table 6.8 *Scenario 1 – effect on distribution of returns*

Returns to deposit holders (IAHs) on average balances		
Depositors' investment accounts	Base case (%)	Scenario case 1 (%)
Saving investment accounts	4.78	3.62
3-months F-PSIA	5.58	4.22
6-months F-PSIA	5.98	4.52
12-months F-PSIA	6.38	4.83
Open-maturity F-PSIA	7.17	5.43
Total returns to investment	6.20	4.69

to the rate-of-return and withdrawal risks by sacrificing shareholder returns to IAHs, which implies a transfer of the risks associated with depositors' accounts to shareholders giving rise to displaced commercial risk. This is one example of how risks can be correlated; however, the bank can be offered mitigation methods to control for rate-of-return risks, as will be elaborated on shortly.

Once risks are identified and understood, for each type of risk an Islamic bank should select, from the various risk measurement methods available, the most suitable approach based on the available data and the nature of the assessed risk. The following section demonstrates the applicable risk measurement methods for each type of risk.

Another important risk to analyse under the effects of varying scenarios is liquidity risk, which is traditionally calculated by measuring maturity gaps. To perform a scenario analysis, each of the three factors that affect the maturity structure of a bank's balance sheet (explained in the previous section) could be altered to provide various scenarios. The three factors are: the maturity structure of assets, the amounts allocated for investment from the different types of deposits and the maturity structure of the invested amounts. Table 6.9 provides an illustrative example of how

Table 6.9 *Change in maturity gaps caused by a shift in the maturity structure of assets (in USD)*

	Maturity gaps based on balance sheet structure			
Maturity	Less than 1 year	From 1 to 5 years	More than 5 years	Total
Assets scenario	30,000,000	25,000,000	45,000,000	100,000,000
case	30%	25%	45%	
base case	24%	43%	33%	
Liabilities	20,363,490	23,308,585	56,327,925	100,000,000
	24%	43%	33%	
Maturity gaps (scenario case)	9,636,510	1,691,415	11,327,925	
Maturity gaps (base case)	–1,200,630	17,804,880	–9,000,000	

a shift in the first factor, the structure of the maturities of assets, leads to a change in the resulting maturity gaps.

Similarly, changing the second and third factors, the amounts invested from each deposited account and the structure of the maturities of the invested amounts, respectively, will also affect the maturity gaps. Increasing the amounts invested (basis for investments) from each investment account by 5 per cent and changing the maturity structures of the invested amounts, as illustrated in Table 6.10, leads to a shift in the maturity gaps, as indicated in Table 6.11. Accordingly, similar simulations can be performed to provide different scenarios and enhance the bank's ability to manage its liquidity position under different conditions.

Other than via the regulatory measures proposed by

Table 6.10 *Scenario analysis of the invested amounts and their maturity structures*

	Basis for investment	5% increase in the basis for investment	Maturity structure of the invested amounts		
			Maturities	Base case	Scenario case
Depositors' investment accounts					
Saving investment accounts	60%	65%	≤ 1 y	20%	25%
			1 y < M ≤ 5 y	45%	30%
			≥ 5 y	35%	45%
			Total	100%	100%
Time deposits					
3-months F-PSIA	70%	75%	≤ 1 y	10%	15%
6-months F-PSIA	75%	80%	1 y < M ≤ 5 y	35%	45%
12-months F-PSIA	80%	85%			
Open-maturity F-PSIA	90%	95%	≥ 5 y	55%	40%
			Total	100%	100%
Shareholders' investments					
Capital	100%	100%	≤ 1 y	40%	60%
Reserves	100%	100%	1 y < M ≤ 5 y	60%	40%
Current accounts and equivalents	40%	45%	≥ 5 y	0%	0%
Mudarib fees	40%		Total	100%	100%

the BIS – the Basic Indicator Approach (BIA) and the Standardised Approach (SA), which are recommended for Islamic banks – operational risk is measured mainly by qualitative methods and may be strengthened by applying

Table 6.11 *Shift in maturity gaps after altering the invested amounts (in USD)*

Maturity gaps based on balance sheet structure				
Maturity	Less than 1 year	From 1 to 5 years	More than 5 years	Total
Assets	24,000,000	43,000,000	33,000,000	100,000,000
Liabilities	25,200,630	25,195,120	42,000,000	
Capital and reserves	0	0	14,000,000	100,000,000
Maturity gaps (scenario case)	−1,200,630	17,804,880	23,000,000	
Maturity gaps (base case)	3,886,510	19,441,415	23,327,925	

scenario-based analyses when required. However, as in conventional banks, operational risk measurement remains a challenging topic, as it is difficult to identify. Hence, it is suggested that Islamic banks should implement an adequate, comprehensive and easy-to-implement monitoring and reporting system in order to minimise operational risks. Moreover, the reported risks should be classified into the different operational risk categories to build an informational database that can be utilised for calculating future operational risk.

The last category of risk to be assessed is business risks. Systemic risk (BRS) and political risk (BRP) are not subject to quantification; however, these risks are evaluated based on market experience as well as economic and political awareness. Hence, it is suggested that a bank's management may analyse these risks by considering the bank's financial position under different economic and political scenarios.

On the other hand, rate-of-return risk (BRR), displaced commercial risk (BRD) and withdrawal risk (BRW) may be quantified subject to suitable data being available. These risks are of relevance to the bank's sources of funds – that is, investment accounts (deposits) and capital – and as such are fundamental for a comprehensive risk analysis process. This is also emphasised by Grais and Kulathunga (2007) who stress the importance of considering investment account deposits, capital, PER and IRR within Islamic banks' comprehensive risk management. Likewise, Sundararajan (2007) specifically illustrates the implications of profit sharing investment accounts (PSIA) for risk measurement and explains that rate-of-return risk is highly dependent on the bank's gross income, as it varies based on deductions attributable to PER, IRR, as well as the bank's *mudarib* share in profits. Accordingly, it is appropriate to identify the variability of such factors within the process of risk assessment.

Rate-of-return risk arises from fluctuations in returns provided to depositors of competitor banks relative to those given to a bank's own depositors (IAHs). Since Islamic banks compete with conventional banks within a global context, the rate-of-return risk should be measured relevant to a market benchmark, such as market interest rates. As such, both gap analysis and duration analysis are applicable measures to quantify rate-of-return risk in Islamic banks. This quantification should be checked by setting different scenarios for possible market interest-rate fluctuations. In addition, other factors that affect the Islamic bank's distribution of returns to its IAHs, such as the bank's profit, PER, *mudarib* fees and IRR, should also be considered within the scenario analysis.

Variability in the rate-of-return risk (BRR) may also lead to withdrawal risk (BRW), which could be calculated from historical fluctuations in depositors' withdrawals.

Additionally, the correlation between the variability of returns and withdrawals could be measured from historical data, to provide an estimate for future withdrawals based on market forecasts. Moreover, in the case of lower returns, a bank's management may choose to transfer part of the shareholder's share of returns to IAHs in order to minimise withdrawal risk. Consequently, the bank is exposed to displaced commercial risk (BRD), which can be assessed provided that the bank holds a relevant historical data set. Otherwise, BRR and BRW would act as indicators for the level of the BRD.

Assume, for example (scenario 2), that the presented Islamic bank witnessed a shocking business year in which the financing income decreased from 8.4 million to 4 million, while investment income and fees and commission income declined from 2.04 million to 1.632 million and from 1.08 million to 0.86 million, respectively, other income realised losses amounting to 0.384 million. The bank increases the impairment provisions to 2.5 million from a previous figure of 2.15 million, and G&A expenses increase to 0.9 million. Accordingly, the bank's net profit and distributions decline by 87 per cent under these assumptions (see Table 6.12).

In this case the bank is highly exposed to business risk, specifically rate-of-return risk and withdrawal risk, since other competitor banks (conventional or Islamic) may be providing better returns to their deposit holders. Assuming that the bank does not hold back amounts of PER and IRR, while having everything else constant, where the bank maintains the same deductions for PER, IRR and *mudarib* fees, returns to IAHs become greatly affected in a way that jeopardises the bank's position in the market. However, in such cases the bank would probably choose to waive its *mudarib* fees in an attempt to provide higher returns for IAHs, which

Table 6.12 *Scenario 2 – effect of a shocking business year on the income statement (in USD)*

Income statement year end 2008		
	Base case	**Scenario case**
Financing income	8,400,000	4,000,000
Investment income	2,040,000	1,632,000
Fees, commissions and foreign exchange income	1,080,000	864,000
Other income	480,000	−384,000
Total operating income	**12,000,000**	**6,112,000**
Employees' costs	−1,250,000	−1,250,000
G&A expenses	−750,000	−900,000
Depreciation	−500,000	−500,000
Provisions for impairment	−2,150,000	−2,500,000
Total operating expenditure	**−4,650,000**	**−5,150,000**
Net profit before PER, IRR and distributions to IHAs	**7,350,000**	**962,000**
PER	−735,000	−96,200
Net profit after PER	**6,615,000**	**865,800**
IRR	−180,906	−23,678
Distributions to deposit holders	−3,437,212	−449,877
Net profit before taxes and *zakah*	**2,996,882**	**392,245**
Average number of shares outstanding	**5,000,000**	**5,000,000**
Earnings per share (EPS)	**0.599**	**0.078**

will in this case increase the distributions to IAHs by 25 per cent, while decreasing returns to shareholders (see Table 6.13). However, the bank can use several methods to smooth out returns to IAHs, as will be elaborated on in the following section.

Liquidity risk is another risk that appears significant in this scenario, where the effect on liquidity levels can be identified by measuring the maturity gaps, as shown in

Table 6.13 *Scenario 2 – effect on profit distributions (in USD)*

	Allocated profit		PER (10%)		Profit after PER		*Mudarib* fees (20%)	
	Base case	Scenario case	Base case	Scenario case	Base case	Scenario case	Base case	Scenario case
Depositors' investment accounts								
Saving investment accounts	1,101,205	144,130	110,120	14,413	991,084	129,717	198,217	25,943
3-months F-PSIA	308,337	40,357	30,834	4,036	277,504	36,321	55,501	7,264
6-months F-PSIA	385,422	50,446	38,542	5,045	346,880	45,401	69,376	9,080
12-months F-PSIA	587,309	76,870	58,731	7,687	528,578	69,183	105,716	13,837
Open-maturity F-PSIA	2,642,891	345,913	264,289	34,591	2,378,602	311,322	475,720	62,264
Total depositors' investment	**5,025,164**	**657,715**	**502,516**	**65,772**	**4,522,648**	**591,944**	**904,530**	**118,389**
Shareholders' investments			**10%**	**10%**				
Capital	1,048,766	137,267	104,877	13,727	943,890	123,540		
Reserves	349,589	45,756	34,959	4,576	314,630	41,180		
Current accounts and equivalent	926,480	121,262	92,648	12,126	833,832	109,136		
Mudarib fees								
Total shareholders	**2,324,836**	**304,285**	**232,484**	**30,428**	**2,092,352**	**273,856**		

Table 6.14. Liquidity levels (in the short term) are highly affected, turning from a positive figure of 3.9 million to a negative figure of 0.5 million, which equates to a 113 per cent decline from the base case. This leads to an increase in liquidity fund-raising risk (LRF), knowing that *Shari'ah*-compliant liquidity management tools are not available for the market yet.

A final and essential step in the assessment process is to

Profit after Mudarib fees		IRR (5%)		Profit after IRR		Returns to IAHs on average balances		
Base case	Scenario case	Base case	Scenario case	Base case	Scenario case	Base case	Scenario case with Mudarib	Scenario case without Mudarib fees
792,867	103,774	39,643	5,189	753,224	98,585	4.78%	0.635	0.78%
222,003	29,057	11,100	1,453	210,903	27,604	5.58%	0.73%	0.91%
277,504	36,321	13,875	1,816	263,628	34,505	5.98%	0.78%	0.98%
422,863	55,346	21,143	2,767	401,720	52,579	6.38%	0.83%	1.04%
1,902,882	249,057	95,144	12,453	1,807,738	236,605	7.17%	0.94%	1.17%
3,618,118	**473,555**	**180,906**	**23,678**	**3,437,212**	**449,877**	**6.20%**	**0.81%**	**1.01%**
943,890	123,540			943,890	123,540			
314,630	41,180			314,630	41,180			
833,832	109,136			833,832	109,136			
904,530	118,389			904,530	118,389			
2,996,882	**392,245**			**2,996,882**	**392,245**	**25%**	**3%**	**2%**

embed the assessed risks within a risk-return performance analysis system and conduct an *ex post* evaluation. The results of the *ex post* evaluation should be further compared with the *ex ante* analysis and targets set prior to the performance phase. As discussed earlier, RAROC is a suitable measure for this purpose.

Following an adequate analysis of risks, suitable mitigation strategies should be determined based on the identified

Table 6.14 *Scenario 2 – effect on maturity gaps*

Maturity gaps based on balance sheet structure				
Maturity	Less than 1 year	From 1 to 5 years	More than 5 years	Total
Assets	19,862,000	42,750,000	33,000,000	95,612,000
	21%	45%	35%	100%
Liabilities	20,363,490	25,308,585	35,939,925	
Capital and	0	0	14,000,000	95,612,000
reserves	21%	26%	38%	100%
Maturity gaps (scenario case)	–501,490	17,441,415	–2,939,925	
Maturity gaps (base case)	3,886,510	19,441,415	–23327925	

risks. The next section illustrates some mitigation methods that could be applied.

6.4 Risk mitigation

Having identified the risks embedded in the presented model, risk mitigation should be conducted. The bank has a set of choices that range between passive and active risk mitigation strategies, as illustrated in Figure 6.4. Active strategies include risk avoidance, reduction and diversification, while passive strategies include risk absorption (financing) and risk transfer methods. As risk transfer methods that comply with *Shari'ah* are still at the research stage and are not yet commonly accepted by the different *Shari'ah* schools, they shall be excluded by the model bank. Hence, the bank will explore the mitigation options offered by active strategies as well as risk absorption.

The first active risk mitigation strategy – risk avoidance – eliminates the probability that a risk will occur, which

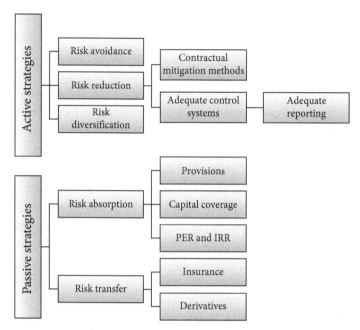

Figure 6.4 *Risk mitigation strategies for Islamic banks*

means that the risk will be eliminated. In this case, this strategy is recommended if a certain risk, when very high, may jeopardise the bank's position if it occurred, which would accordingly require the risk to be avoided. In our example, the bank applied this strategy by avoiding contract engagements in *musharakah*, and minimising *mudaraba* engagements to 3 per cent, as both types of contracts are viewed as highly risky. In fact, deviating away from providing high-risk financing tools such as *musharaka* and *mudaraba* is a common practice in Islamic banks. In practice, most Islamic banks tend to deviate away from financing or investing in unsecured projects or industries, thus adopting a risk avoidance strategy at large. Consequently, this strategy results in them having a conservative business model and hence, not vulnerable to systemic shocks.

Risk reduction methods are those strategies that minimise the severity of loss. These include the contractual risk mitigation methods presented in section 5.2. Thus, by analysing the balance sheet structure of the bank and identifying the contracted financing tools, the bank should adopt the mitigation methods required for each type of contract. Another type of risk reduction is having adequate control systems in place, which includes implementing an adequate reporting system that involves standardisation and building up an informational platform. An adequate control system should be embedded within a bank's management policy, developed through its top management and passed through to lower level management for implementation and feedback. The BIS emphasises the importance of adopting an adequate control system, specifically for credit risk, in which banks should establish an independent ongoing credit risk assessment, an efficient and effective monitoring system, and enforce internal controls (BCBS 2000a: 1–4). Currently, control systems go beyond credit risk and are considered the backbone of risk management systems, especially for managing operational risks. Ahmed (2010) highlights the importance of developing adequate internal control systems as a main element in establishing a risk management system in banks. Similarly, Cunningham (2004) states that if Islamic banks operate as part of the global financial system they must adhere to global reporting standards.

Two primary factors inherent within effective internal controls are to adopt risk limits and to ensure regular and adequate reporting. Risk limits should be set and monitored by the bank's top management. Furthermore, a bank's management should identify a reporting framework that can be easily followed. A risk reporting framework requires some standardisation within the Islamic banking business and a separation of the risk management functions within a bank.

The AAOIFI is putting considerable effort into establishing common guidelines for the industry to be adopted worldwide and to thus provide standardisation within the industry. Ahmed (2010) suggests that the separation of risk identification, measurement, mitigation and review units must be ensured for appropriate risk management.

Similarly, in order to manage equity investment risk some essential factors should be considered: regular independent monitoring and auditing of risks, effective communication (reporting and documentation), training of employees, implementing an incentive system to encourage a safe attitude, and a penalty system for repeated violation of risk control policies and procedures (Mohamed and Kayed 2007). Ismal (2010) reveals that Islamic banks in Malaysia basically manage their liquidity by setting appropriate strategies for equity and debt financing that are regularly monitored and reported. Consequently, adequate risk reporting and monitoring allows for a broad mitigation of risks that is made easy in a standardised environment.

However, in spite of the importance of standardisation, Chapra (2007) stipulates that it should only be taken so far, so that some differences of opinion are allowed to remain; hence, allowing different alternatives for doing business and financial innovations rather than imposing a totally rigid set of standards. Standardisation can be achieved by having a centralised *Shari'ah* board instead of a large number of *Shari'ah* boards each heading an Islamic financial institution and providing conflicting opinions. Yet, the centralised *Shari'ah* board should be open to differences of opinion. In this regard, the AAOIFI (2008) published *Shari'ah* standards that include the different opinions (interpretations) of *Shari'ah* scholars, where they exist. Moreover, in an attempt to standardise Islamic financial contracts and accounting disclosures, the *Shari'ah* and accounting standards are supported by the AAOIFI accounting, auditing and governance standards.

Yet, having a centralised *Shari'ah*-standard-setting institution does not in itself ensure that Islamic banks implement their transactions in conformity with *Shari'ah*. Hence, similar to external auditing that ensures appropriate conformity with accounting standards, a *Shari'ah* clearance or audit is essential to ensure conformity with the stipulated standards. Chapra (2007) suggests that *Shari'ah* audit/clearance can be performed either by supervisory authorities, independent *Shari'ah* audit firms or existing chartered audit firms after acquiring the necessary knowledge and expertise in *Shari'ah*. Moreover, in order to facilitate regular and adequate risk reporting, an effective informational platform should be facilitated. To this end, the presented coding system is recommended for application to build a suitable risk management framework for Islamic banks that ensures and facilitates reporting and monitoring of risks. Adequate risk reporting will eventually provide a suitable database that should solve the quantification problem in Islamic banks.

The third active mitigation strategy, risk diversification, minimises the end result of the risk by diversifying the events of uncertainty. This entails diversification of the bank's investment portfolio so that the bank is involved in less-risky activities, such as debt-based financing, as well as more-risky activities, such as PLS financing, (see the presented balance sheet structure as an example). Also, banks may implement a diversification strategy to minimise each risk *per se*; for instance, to minimise credit risk a bank may diversify its portfolio of assets by investing in different geographical areas and different sectors. Likewise, one method to diversify market (equity) risk is to invest in different trading portfolios.

Contrary to active strategies, passive strategies do not involve a change in either the consequence or the probability of the risk. Instead, passive mitigation strategies accept that a certain risk could occur and utilise covering funds to mitigate the risk as it occurs. Risk absorption is the first passive mitigation strategy. Under risk absorption a bank's management identifies methods, such as using capital reserves and annual profits, which would cover certain amounts of risk. Khan (2004) illustrates that an Islamic bank should use income to cover expected losses from provisions, while unexpected losses should be covered by PER, IRR and capital reserves. However, extreme unexpected losses would be better covered through *takaful* (Islamic insurance), which is one method of the risk transfer strategy.

It is worth noting that PER and IRR are not only used for covering losses, but should also be utilised to smooth out returns and mitigate other risks when a bank faces low profits. Consider, for example, the second scenario assumed in section 6.3 (see p. 154), in which the bank faced a shocking business year where the financing income decreased from 8.4 million to 4 million. In this scenario, the bank can undertake two actions in order to smooth returns to IAHs during that year. First, no deductions for PER, IRR and/or *mudarib* fees should be considered from IAHs or shareholders during this year. In this case, if the bank does not deduct PER, IRR and *mudarib* fees, the distribution of returns to IAHs will increase by 32 per cent, reaching 1.19 per cent from 0.81 per cent, on average, as shown in Table 6.15. If the bank chooses to exclude deductions for *mudarib* fees while maintaining the deduction strategy for PER and IRR, then distributions to IAHs will fall to 1.01 per cent, on average. Second, the bank has the option to utilise previous deductions of PER and IRR to increase returns distributed to IAHs as well as shareholders. These two actions will

Table 6.15 Scenario 2 – *risk mitigation through PER and IRR*

	Distribution of returns on average balances			
	Base case (%)	Scenario case with *mudarib* fees (%)	Scenario case without *mudarib* fees (%)	Scenario case without *mudarib* fees, PER and IRR (%)
Depositors' investment accounts				
Saving investment accounts	4.78	0.63	0.78	0.92
3-months F-PSIA	5.58	0.73	0.91	1.07
6-months F-PSIA	5.98	0.78	0.98	1.14
12-months F-PSIA	6.38	0.83	1.04	1.22
Open-maturity F-PSIA	7.17	0.94	1.17	1.37
Total depositors' investment	**6.20**	**0.81**	**1.01**	**1.19**
Total shareholders' investment	**25**	**3**	**2**	**3**

increase the distribution of returns and thus minimise BRW and BRD.

This scenario also clarifies the exposure to liquidity risk. As stated earlier, the sources of liquidity risk for Islamic banks are the same as for conventional banks, but the mitigation methods available for liquidity management in Islamic banks are limited. Hence, liquidity risk management represents a major challenge for Islamic banks, basically due to the absence of a lender of last resort and the lack of an internationally recognised liquidity infrastructure.

Therefore, this area requires further research and coopera-tion among researchers and practitioners.

Some attempts to address these problems are worth men-tioning. Three liquidity centres have been established. The first, the Liquidity Management Center (LMC) in Bahrain, has been established to manage short- and medium-term liquidity mismatch in Islamic financial institutions in accordance with *Shari'ah* principles, by creating an Islamic interbank market and launching securitised assets and innovative investment instruments.[5] In addition, Bursa Malaysia's *Suq al-Sila'* has been introduced as another attempt to solve the problems of commodity *murabaha* (*tawarruq*). Dusuki (2010) explains that Bursa Malaysia have designed a platform to facilitate *tawarruq*, what is referred to as a 'Commodity *Murabaha* House platform'. However, the instruments used within this have not been approved by *Shari'ah* scholars in the Gulf. More recently, global Islamic liquidity management cooperation has been initiated by eleven central banks under the auspices of the IFSB (Reuters 2010). Whether such attempts will solve the liquidity management problem for Islamic banks or not will be demonstrated over time.

To conclude, an Islamic bank has a wide set of strate-gies available to mitigate various risks and achieve high returns. Yet risk mitigation tools, and specifically the risk transfer strategies, require further research before they are accepted by the various schools of *Shari'ah*. As stated ear-lier, the second phase within a risk management framework is ensuring that risk regulation has been met, but Islamic banks do not yet have a clear set of international banking regulations. The next chapter provides a discussion of inter-national risk management regulation and the prospects for Islamic banks.

Notes

1. The six largest Islamic banks are Kuwait Finance House (KFH), Dubai Islamic Bank (DIB), Abu-Dhabi Islamic Bank (ADIB), Al-Rajhi Bank, Qatar Islamic Bank (QIB) and Al-Baraka Bank.

2. This case study has been verified with AbdelKabir El-Batanoni, an expert in Islamic banking having been an Islamic bank consultant for over 20 years.

3. Based on Abozaid (2008) and Dusuki (2010), the practice of commodity *murabaha* and *tawarruq* does not conform to the permissible definition of *tawarruq* and thus organised *tawarruq* was condemned as unacceptable by the OIC *Fiqh* Academy. For a further discussion of this, refer to A. Abozaid (2010), 'Towards genuine *Shari'ah* products with lessons of the financial crisis', and A. Dusuki (2010), 'Can Bursa Malaysia's *Suq al-Sila*' resolve the controversy over *Tawarruq*?', papers presented at a conference on Islamic Finance and Financial Crisis, Durham, UK, 14–15 July, 2010.

4. For further insights about the financial analysis of Islamic banks amid the crisis, see Salem and Badreldin (2010).

5. Retrieved on 4 August 2010, from http://www.lmcbahrain.com/role.asp.

CHAPTER 7
PROSPECTS FOR RISK REGULATION IN ISLAMIC BANKS

The banking industry applies prudent regulations on the domestic and international level, of which regulating the underlying risks is a fundamental objective. Meyer (2000) states that risk management contributes to market discipline through effective banking supervision, which ensures that a bank's performance is assessed and the required adjustments for its loan loss provisions made. Risk regulation varies from one country to another; however, since the business of banking extends over the global arena, banks seek to follow international risk regulations – and Islamic banks are no exception. To date, an Islamic banking regulatory framework has not been completely developed and financial institutions offering Islamic financial services are required to cooperate to resolve regulatory issues to ensure sustainability of the industry. As a result of operating in a dual banking system, it is vital that Islamic banks ensure their compliance to regulatory requirements. Consequently, and since risk regulation is one of the most important aspects of banking regulations – while at the same time recognising that the regulatory framework needed for Islamic banks would differ from that of conventional banks – the viability of adapting Basel II, and now Basel III, to the Islamic banking system is discussed. This chapter describes the international risk management regulations with a brief illustration of the three pillars of Basel II and highlights of Basel III. Also, the proposed risk regulations for Islamic banks, IFSB and Basel II/III, as well as the challenges of adapting Basel II/III to Islamic banks are discussed.

7.1 Risk management regulation

Events in the international banking market raised the fear of systemic risk: the risk of a failure in the banking system resulting from individual banks' risks (Bessis 2002). This fear created the need for an internationally recognised financial regulator, which resulted in the setting up of the Bank for International Settlements (BIS; McIlroy 2008). The BIS identified risk management among the core principles for setting sound supervisory practices designed to improve financial stability and strengthen the global financial system (Heffernan 2005; BCBS 2006b: 112–13). In addition, the Basel Capital Accord was introduced by the BIS to ensure the efficiency of banks' risk management and support the confidence of market participants in the banking system through proposing adequate principles and methods of a 'best practice' risk management framework (McNeil *et al.* 2005; Al-Tamimi and Al-Mazrooei 2007; BCBS 2009). These risk management principles stress the importance of setting minimum capital adequacy requirements and of having a comprehensive risk management process. They also address having adequate policies in place to identify, measure, control and monitor credit, market, liquidity and operational risks, where the policies required for managing operational risk depend greatly on the complexity and size of the bank.

International risk management regulation was initiated in 1988 when the first Basel Accord was introduced, which was concerned with credit risk measurement; that had been a challenge due to the lack of reliable inputs. Later, in 1996, amendments that provided a standardised approach for market risk measurement were added to the Accord. These amendments recommended that the minimum capital requirement for market risk should be quantified based on the Value at Risk (VaR) approach (Marrison 2002). In addition, the amendments called for banks to implement a risk management framework that integrated with daily risk management, specifically for setting trading limits and risk monitoring (Crouhy *et al.* 2001: 47).

The Basel II Accord was then introduced in 2001, and implemented in 2004, to enhance credit risk measurement, extend operational risk into capital requirements and put emphasis on a bank's internal methodologies and market transparency. This Accord aimed to produce a higher level of financial system stability and encompasses three pillars (see Figure 7.1): pillar 1 focuses on minimum capital requirements, pillar 2 reviews the supervisory process and pillar 3 promotes market discipline (Bessis 2002). More recently, in response to the sub-prime financial crisis, the Basel III Accord was introduced to the market aiming for a safer financial system through strengthening capital and liquidity standards in the banking sector worldwide. This new Accord is designed to increase the required level and quality of banks' capital on one hand, and on the other to introduce new global minimum liquidity standards. Amendments relevant to capital standards include: considering common equity and retained earnings among Tier 1 capital, simplifying harmonised requirements for Tier 2 capital, increasing minimum required capital to 10.5 per cent from 8 per cent, and setting a leverage limit at 3 per cent. As regards to the amendments relevant to liquidity standards, two regulatory liquidity standards – namely, liquidity coverage ratio and net stable funding ratio – will be introduced in 2015 and

2018, respectively. The former ratio addresses the liquidity risk arising from shortage of liquid assets, while the latter addresses the balance sheet mismatching risk (Caruana 2010; Cecchetti 2010). The amendments introduced through Basel III underline the importance of capturing risk appropriately: emphasis has been given to the quality of modelling counterparty credit risk, the existing correlation among financial institutions, and the quality of collaterals and stress testing as tools for managing risk (KPMG 2011).

From the history of the Basel Accord, it is clear that supervisory frameworks are dynamic and respond to global economic and financial changes. International supervisory authorities, such as the Basel Accord, were originally set up to enable both Islamic and conventional banks to mitigate risks in a similar manner (Fiennes 2007). Sundararajan (2007: 40–64) suggests that an effective supervision of Islamic banks should call for appropriately adapting the three-pillar framework of Basel II to their unique operational characteristics. To this end, the Islamic Financial Services Board (IFSB), an international standard-setting organisation, provides invaluable standards adapted from Basel II standards for all Islamic banks with regard to risk management and capital adequacy. The IFSB aims at promoting the financial stability and soundness of the Islamic banking system and smoothes its integration into the conventional financial system by setting globally accepted standards.

Regulators require conventional banks, which are characterised by being highly leveraged, to keep a minimum capital requirement that acts as a buffer in case of losses. The 'capital adequacy',[1] which represents the first and main pillar of the regulatory scheme in limiting risk failure, is to provide protection against unexpected losses, while leaving average/expected losses covered by traditional provisions

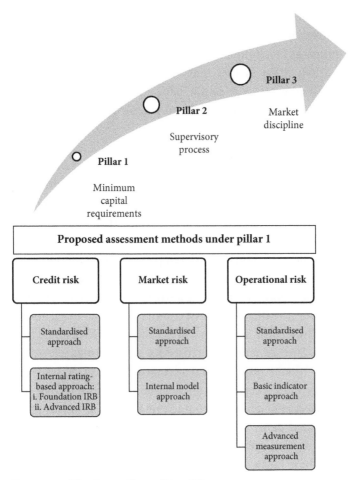

Figure 7.1 *The three pillars of Basel II*

and reserves. The higher the risk banks take, the more capital they are required to maintain on their balance sheet, otherwise banks would find difficulty in raising funds (Heffernan 2005). Likewise, Rosman (2008) points out that maintaining adequate capital is also important to Islamic banks because it indicates the quality of the banks' liabilities. However, the unique characteristics of Islamic banks' assets and the restrictions imposed by *Shari'ah* principles regarding risk mitigation techniques (such as guarantees and derivatives) are two main factors that affect the calculation of risk-weighted assets for Islamic banks, causing risk weights to vary between conventional and Islamic banks (Archer and Abdel Karim 2007: 223–35).

Defining the capital level that protects a bank against losses is the basic principle of 'capital adequacy' and entails quantitative assessment of risks. This requires valuing risks as compared to a bank's capital base and adjusting the level of capital to match the valued risks. This highlights the importance of setting risk limits or tolerance levels. Risk quantification models are developed to investigate and value the potential losses arising from all risks against capital. As a basic component for having a strong risk management programme, the BIS identifies a comprehensive internal assessment for capital adequacy (BCBS 2009: 9). 'The capital base equals 8 per cent of weighted assets' is sometimes referred to as the 'Cooke ratio'; capital adequacy is measured by dividing the bank's capital by an asset-base measure of risk. The banks' capital consists of equity, retained earnings and subordinated debt. The regulatory capital requirement covers market risk, credit risk and operational risk within the asset-base measure of risk (Crouhy *et al.* 2001: 71–96; Bessis 2002: 35–50; Freeland and Friedman 2007: 215–22). Hence, adequate measurement of the underlying risks should be considered before deciding on the asset-base measure of the Capital Adequacy Ratio (CAR). The BIS also proposed alternative methods for quantifying credit, operational and market risks.

For credit risk measurement, the BIS proposed the Internal-Rating-Based approach (IRB) and the standardised approach. The IRB is an internal rating assessment of the credit facilities provided by the bank by estimating the bank's probability of default (PD), loss given default (LGD), the exposure at default (EAD) and the loan maturity. The BIS provides two types of IRB approaches: the foundation approach, in which banks account only for the PD; and the advanced approach, in which banks estimate all the credit risk components (BCBS 2006b; Curcio and Gianfrancesco 2010). The second assessment method is the standardised approach, which calculates risk weights of assets based on the credit worthiness of counterparties. The standardised approach is simpler than the IRB approach, which calculates the risk capital by measuring the riskiness of a bank's credit exposures (McNeil *et al.* 2005: 11–12; BCBS 2006b).

With regard to operational risk, the Basel Committee is concerned with losses resulting from internal processes, people and systems, or those resulting from external events. Despite acknowledging the fact that operational risk measurement is crucial to financial risk management, it is very difficult to agree on a specific method to quantify such risks or to what extent they should be considered (McNeil *et al.* 2005). The BIS proposes the Basic Indicator Approach (BIA), the standardised approach, and the Advanced Measurement Approach (AMA) to assess operational risk. The BIA simply requires banks to set aside a certain percentage of capital for operational risk, and thus is recommended only for banks with no international exposures. The standardised (operational) approach measures operational risk of a bank based on the performance of the bank's business lines, while the AMA is considered the most complex operational risk measure in which banks are allowed to develop their own empirical measurement methods (BCBS 2006c).

The BIS also provides two market risk assessment approaches – pertaining to interest-rate-related instruments, equities, foreign exchange and commodities risks

– that remain unchanged from the 1996 Basel I amendments. The first is the internal model approach, which uses models that capture valuation, sensitivity and correlation effects, and the second the simple standardised approach. It is worth mentioning that commodity risks embedded within market risk are more complex to assess, as they combine price risk with other risks (Bessis 2002). Commodity (price) risk, elaborated on shortly, is one of the commonly identified risks in Islamic banks (such as that associated with *salam* and *murabaha* contracts) which clarifies the difficulty of measuring Islamic banking market risks. Archer and Abdel Karim (2007: 223–35) reveal that measuring capital adequacy for Islamic banks is considered a challenging aspect because of the difficulty in calculating market and credit risks.

Similarly, the IFSB issued a capital adequacy standard[2] specifically directed towards Islamic banks and based on the Basel II standardised approach. The standard gives the same risk weight for Islamic banks provided that hybrid capital and subordinated debts are not included in the bank's equity. The PER attributable to IAHs and the IRR are also excluded from capital; since both act as a buffer protecting IAHs from low returns and future investment risks, respectively, they should be taken into account when measuring risk-weighted assets (Grais and Kulathunga 2007: 69–93).

The second pillar, the supervisory review process, ensures that individual banks possess adequate internal processes to evaluate and assess their capital base as compared to risks in order to strengthen capital adequacy standards. The proposed enhancements to Basel II (BCBS 2009) suggest that capital under the second pillar should exceed the minimum capital requirement under the first pillar, to guarantee that both on- and off-balance-sheet risks are adequately covered.

Finally, the third pillar strengthens the role of capital markets, by suggesting that market discipline and comprehensive disclosure among market participants are main factors in reinforcing capital regulation and promoting soundness of the financial system (Bessis 2002).

Having a clear international regulatory framework is important but there can be some drawbacks to regulation. For example, regulators are concerned with the overall riskiness of a bank over a time horizon rather than the individual portfolio risk. Ignoring a bank's intraday total risks could lead some managers to 'window dress' a bank's position in order to meet regulatory requirements, which would impose more risks to the financial system (Pyle 1997: 5). The high cost of setting up a compliant well-established risk management framework and the capital requirements that might contribute to a liquidity dry in times of crises are two highly critical points of regulation. Another disadvantage embedded within setting regulations is the lack of transparency and regulatory arbitrage that arises with complex regulatory requirements. Meeting regulatory requirements may reveal other financial risks through motivating financial innovations. For instance, banks responded to the first Basel Capital Accord (Basel I) by securitising loans, which allowed banks to transfer the loans off their balance sheets through bundling up and selling the loans, in order to open more credit opportunities for the bank. A similar approach has contributed to the recent sub-prime crisis that started in the United States and rapidly spread through the international financial market (McIlroy 2008).

Accordingly, providing a credible assessment method that measures capital adequacy within the innovative nature of financial markets and the large variety of financial instruments and risks has become a major challenge. The recent crisis has shown that the currently practised risk regulations require further modifications. The barriers that limit risks disappear in the event of bank failures, when aggressive risk-taking actions are practised in the hope of maximising chances of survival. Consequently, Mcllroy (2008) suggests that regulators should force banks to keep some of the risks embedded within their business in their book, in order to ensure risk transparency and minimise banks' moral hazard, which accompanies the process of securitisation. Risk transparency means that a trading instrument should not be allowed unless its underlying risks have been analysed.

The importance of regulating banking risks has indeed been recognised, but the current regulatory risk management scheme reveals significant shortcomings. Scholes (2000) suggests that risk management models and capital cushions should be dynamic to be less prone to difficulties in financial crises. Accordingly, risk management regulation is to be revisited by researchers, regulators and industry experts to provide flexible regulations that adapt to the dynamic nature of the financial system, such as the introduction of Basel III after the sub-prime financial crisis. When regulating risk management under the Islamic banking system, even more work would be required than for the conventional system, for two reasons. First, risk management in Islamic banks requires a clear infrastructure or framework based on an adequate understanding of the business model and the underlying risks. Second, the attempts at setting an internationally agreed-upon risk-management regulatory framework have not yet been productive – despite the efforts of the IFSB, which have issued risk management guidelines as well as capital adequacy standards, amongst others, for Islamic financial institutions.

7.2 Risk management regulation status quo

Regulating risks in Islamic banks is critical to maintain sustainability, contribute to market discipline and minimise systemic risk. The International Monetary Fund (IMF) conducted a study to examine the contribution of banks to financial stability, which revealed that small Islamic banks maintain the highest degree of financial stability, followed by large conventional banks. To the contrary though, large Islamic banks were perceived to have the lowest degree of financial stability because of their limited ability to adjust credit risk monitoring systems to their diverse set of products (Heiko and Cihak 2008). Hence, regulators of Islamic banks are also directed to the importance of addressing an appropriate level of capital to limit systemic risks. In practice, Islamic banks operate in diverse regulatory systems and may be subject to different supervisory regulations, yet the need to protect individual consumers is a common goal among supervisors from different regimes (Archer and Abdel Karim 2007: 223–35). Another regulatory role of importance for Islamic banks is ensuring and monitoring the compliance of banks offering Islamic products with *Shari'ah* principles (Fiennes 2007: 247–56). This role requires supervisors to maintain the appropriate knowledge and skills, as well as taking on an authoritative function.

An Islamic banking regulatory framework has not been fully developed to date and financial institutions offering Islamic financial services need to cooperate to resolve the regulatory issues and ensure sustainability of the industry. According to Khan and Bhatti (2008), Dubai Financial Services Authority, the IFSB and Malaysia's Securities, among others, have been cooperating with conventional banking authorities on resolving regulatory issues related to Islamic banking and finance. As a result of operating in a dual banking system, it is vital that Islamic banks ensure their compliance to regulatory requirements. Since risk regulation is one of the most important aspects of banking regulations, while recognising that the regulatory framework required by Islamic banks would differ from that of conventional banks (Greuning and Iqbal 2008), the viability of adapting Basel II to the Islamic banking system has been discussed throughout the literature. Some governments are also following the same methodology: the Kuwaiti government has initiated a project to adapt Basel II for Islamic banks. In addition, the IFSB have proposed risk management guidelines and capital adequacy requirements similar to those issued by the Bank for International Settlements (BIS). This section explains the proposed risk regulations for Islamic banks, IFSB and Basel II, discusses the challenges of adapting Basel II to Islamic banks and highlights the possible implications of Basel III for Islamic banks.

The IFSB guidelines (2005a) represent the pioneering efforts to regulate risk management for Islamic banks by providing risk management guidelines and capital adequacy standards that are adopted from Basel II. The guidelines cover six types of risks, namely credit, equity investment, market, liquidity, rate of return and operational, and stipulate that financial institutions that offer Islamic financial services should comply with *Shari'ah* rules when applying risk management principles. It is also noted that Islamic banks should recognise and evaluate the mix of the above-mentioned risks, as well as other risks such as reputational, business and *Shari'ah* compliance. In addition, as a general requirement, a comprehensive risk management process that complies with *Shari'ah* principles should be maintained for every risk. However, unlike the Basel Accord, the IFSB does not provide specific guidance on the appropriate components for the capital base, and also the IFSB standards are not implemented globally. For example, in the UK, the Financial Services Authority (FSA) – the country's financial regulator – treats Islamic and conventional transactions under the same guidelines, rather than applying the IFSB guidelines (Schoon 2008).

Specifically for credit risk, and as a result of the restrictions imposed on penalties and collaterals within the context of Islamic banks, the guidelines emphasise the importance of an adequate assessment of counterparties. Also, appropriate measurement, reporting and mitigation techniques should be put in place (IFSB 2005a). On the abstract level, such guidelines appear to be similar to those for conventional credit-risk management. However, because the degree of credit risk varies for different products as a result of the changing nature of the contractual relationship at different stages of the contract, the IFSB adds that a separate credit risk assessment should take place for each financial instrument (Akkizidis and Khandelwal 2008). A similar process is suggested for equity investment risk, where Islamic banks should properly evaluate the risk and manage it through identifying exit strategies. Since equity risks arise particularly from PLS activities such as *mudarba* and *musharaka*, all the related strategies should be mutually agreed upon among counterparties before engaging in the contract. The guidelines proposed for market, liquidity, rate-of-return and operational risks suggest having an appropriate risk management framework that includes identifying risk exposures, determining mitigation methods and reporting risk positions. Furthermore, the IFSB generally stresses the importance of *Shari'ah*-compliant risk mitigation techniques wherever appropriate (IFSB 2005a).

Schoon (2008) sums up the main challenges to applying Basel II in Islamic banks. First, Islamic banks lack the appropriate databases to determine the adequate capital, since the industry's loan-loss history does not represent a significant sample size. It is worth noting that the application of Basel II varies according to the availability of historical data and models used in calculating a bank's adequate capital. Second, the risk profile of Islamic banks is different from that of conventional banks and thus requires special modifications. For instance, conventional banks are penalised for holding higher equity positions by assigning a higher risk weight to meet the capital adequacy requirements. Therefore, Islamic banks should be cautious in financing through *musharaka* and *mudaraba*, which are equity-based modes. Hence, developing standards aimed specifically at Islamic banks is inevitable.

Regulating risk management for Islamic banks requires more work to meet international regulatory requirements, specifically in adopting the first pillar of Basel II. As for the second pillar, the recommendations of the Basel committee reveal that it is generally applicable to Islamic banks, but it should be recognised that managing liquidity risk remains a challenge to Islamic banks and that the present recommendations appear insufficient in the absence of supporting risk management models. Similarly, the third pillar, which stresses the importance of market disclosure, is a challenging topic for the Islamic banking industry in the absence of standardised financial reporting and comparable information, since the AAOIFI accounting standards are not mandatory. However, it is worth mentioning that transparency, which is also an important element of market discipline, is at the core of Islamic financial contracts and is thus widely applied in Islamic banks (Akkizidis and Khandelwal 2008).

Setting minimum capital requirements fulfils the first pillar of Basel II. Basically, conventional banks are required to maintain a minimum capital (Tier 1, Tier 2 and Tier 3)[3] of 8 per cent of the risk-adjusted assets under Basel II, currently increased to 10 per cent based on Basel III amendments. Chapra and Khan (2000) propose that maintaining capital requirements will help ensure the credibility of Islamic banks worldwide. In general, capital adequacy requirements (CAR) are irrelevant to Islamic banks as they do not work for investment deposits (accounts) that are mobilised on the basis of profit-and-loss sharing (Abdel Karim 1996). While Islamic banks are expected to have Tier 1 capital characteristics similar to those of regular banks, Tier 2 capital requirements appear problematic considering that the components of Tier 2 – interest-bearing capital such as hybrid capital instruments or subordinated debts – are not allowed by *Shari'ah* principles (Greuning and Iqbal 2008). Accordingly, capital requirements for Islamic banks should vary from those of their conventional counterparts. Hence, taking into consideration the implications of Basel III, under which capital requirements have been modified to the 10.5 per cent level, further research and cooperation between regulatory and supervisory authorities and Islamic banks should be established to determine appropriate capital requirements. However, in practice, Islamic banks tend to maintain high levels of capital that in most cases reach the 10.5 per cent regulatory level and would, therefore, appear compatible with their conventional counterparts.

It is sometimes argued, however, that Islamic financial institutions have inherently larger capital requirements because of the liquidity management challenge they face: Islamic banks lack money-market instruments, interbank activities and secondary markets. Accordingly, it is suggested that the required capital level should be set higher for Islamic banks than their conventional counterparts, since the PLS arrangements do not allow the enforcement of collaterals, a key factor in controlling credit risk, its absence increasing credit risk exposure (Makiyan 2008).

The supervisory authorities should perhaps set the capital level for each individual bank based on its risk profile and the adequacy of its risk management process, which to date is not the case. Chapra and Khan (2000) propose a segregation of capital adequacy treatments for both current deposits and profit-sharing investment accounts (PSIA; investment deposits), since current deposit holders require more protection than investment deposit holders who share bank risks with shareholders (equity capital). Moreover, Obaidullah (1998) recommends that since investment deposits hold the feature of absorbing losses, they can be included as a component of capital. According to Muljawan *et al.* (2004), the same suggestion was supported by the AAOIFI's approach to capital regulation.

In the statement issued by the AAOIFI on 'The purpose and calculation of the Capital Adequacy Ratio for Islamic banks' in March 1999, three factors should be considered when calculating the capital adequacy ratio (CAR; which should equal at least 8%). First, investment accounts based on profit sharing should not be included in the risk-bearing capital. Second, the denominator of the CAR is to include all assets financed through debt-based liabilities and equity. Finally, to cover possible losses arising from the negligence of the management, 50 per cent of profit-sharing investment financed assets should be added to the denominator. Hence, the final equation for calculating the CAR is as follows (Muljawan *et al.* 2004):

$$CAR = \frac{OC}{W_{OC+L} \, (OC + L) + W_{PSIA} \, (0.5 * PSIA)}$$

where OC is the bank's own capital, L is the non-PLS deposits, W represents average risk weights and PSIA are assets financed by profit-sharing investment accounts.

Abdel Karim (1996) presents the impact of four possible scenarios for the treatment of PSIA within the CAR on Islamic banks' financial strategies. The first scenario assumes that PSIAs are added to the core capital (Tier 1), which implies that Islamic banks would easily be able to meet capital requirements. The second scenario, where the PSIAs are assumed to be deducted from total risk-weighted assets, holds true when the CAR is increased as a result of a reduction in the total risk-weighted assets. The third scenario stipulates that PSIAs are added as an extra element to Tier 2 capital, which means that Islamic banks would face difficulties in maintaining the CAR requirements. The third scenario supports the view that PSIAs do not perfectly substitute for equity, which is permanently available; instead PSIAs resemble hybrid capital instruments without an obligation to distribute returns. The final scenario is that the Basel framework is applied without adjustments for PSIAs. In this case, Islamic banks should increase equity capital or restructure assets to reach lower risk weightings.

According to the Basel Accord, identifying what is adequate capital requires a quantification of the underlying credit, market and operational risks (weight of risky assets). In addition, the assessment of capital adequacy for Islamic banks should be based on an evaluation of the mix of PLS and sale-based assets, as suggested by Sundararajan and Errico (2002), since the degree of risk for PLS assets varies from that of sale-based assets. PLS assets are known to be more risky than sale-based assets, and thus would require a higher capital adequacy ratio. Hence, the overall risk will depend on both the weight of risky assets and the mix of risks on the balance sheet.

Chapra and Khan (2000) argue that the best method for measuring risk weights in Islamic banks is the internal based approach (IRB), as it allows banks to follow their own developed risk management system and identify the probability of default for each asset separately. However, Akkizidis and Khandelwal (2008) suggest that the standardised and IRB approaches require several amendments before employing them to Islamic banks, since some risks, such as credit risk, are dynamic and arise at different intervals in Islamic banks' contracts.

In a more detailed analysis, Jabbari (2006) suggests that for credit risk measurement, when external credit ratings are available, the standardised approach is applicable; for PLS modes, a simple risk-weight method (risk weights of 300% or 400%) or a slotting method can be used. The 'supervisory slotting criteria' are suggested by Basel II for banks that do not meet the requirements when estimating the probability of default (PD) for their corporate exposures. Such banks are requested to map their specialised lending assets into five supervisory categories, each associated with a specific risk weight (Lifen 2008). For identifying the credit risk weight that should be assigned, the resulting risk weights are then multiplied by the net exposures adjusted for available collaterals (Figure 7.2).

As regards to market risk weights, the standardised market and internal models approaches used for quantifying market risk, based on Basel II, are not directly applicable to Islamic banks (Akkizidis and Khandelwal 2008). Market risk in Islamic banks varies from that of conventional banks in two ways: it includes high concentrations of commodity price risk and mark-up/benchmark risk replaces interest rate risk. Also, a new category of risk, equity risk, is added for Islamic banks in the presence of PLS modes of financing. Thus, the IFSB provides a framework similar to that of Basel II, but includes commodity price risk and equity risk in the measurement of weights, while focusing on the standardised approach (Figure 7.3).

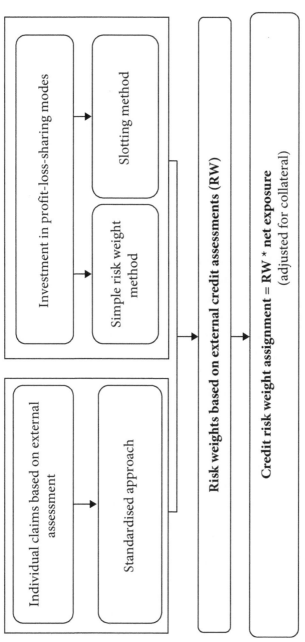

Figure 7.2 *Framework for measuring credit risk weights. Source: Jabbari (2006), as cited in Greuning and Iqbal (2008)*

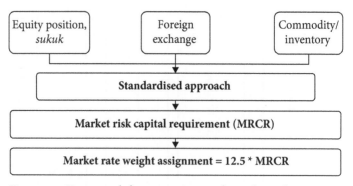

Figure 7.3 *Framework for measuring market risk weights. Source: Jabbari (2006), as cited in Greuning and Iqbal (2008: 229)*

Akkizidis and Khandelwal (2008: 96) acknowledge that the weights allocated by the BIS for measuring operating risk do not represent the true operational risk exposures for Islamic banks, where they are expected to be higher and more complex than in conventional banks. In Islamic banks, operational risk exposures vary during the life time of the contract and hence a standard weight is not applicable.

It can be concluded that a risk management regulatory framework for Islamic banks is not fully developed yet; the problems of determining the adequate level of capital, the appropriate components of the CAR and a suitable framework for measuring risk weights need to be resolved and agreed upon on the international level. Additionally, with the recent sub-prime crisis, current European debt crisis, and structural, regulatory (presented in Basel III) and institutional changes in the global banking industry, the need for a well-developed regulatory framework for Islamic banks is more challenging, yet more important.

A critical challenge that faces Islamic banks in the context of international regulation is their ability to meet regulatory liquidity standards. On the one hand, is the liquidity management challenge faced by Islamic banks as a result of the lack of liquid assets and a well-structured money market with *Shari'ah*-compliant instruments, and, on the other, are the new liquidity requirements imposed by Basel III. Of the two introduced measures for assessing liquidity risk, the liquidity coverage ratio appears more critical than the net stable funding ratio. The liquidity coverage ratio aims at promoting resilience to short-term liquidity distortions by measuring liquidity coverage for a 30-day period. With the absence of *Shari'ah*-compliant money-market tools, adhering to this measure is highly challenged for Islamic banks. On the other hand, the net stable funding ratio appears less challenging as it basically encourages banks to maintain stable sources to fund their activities rather than depending on short-term funds. This liquidity measure might turn out to benefit Islamic banks as, theoretically speaking, they should already be less dependent on short-term funds since there is a shortage of *Shari'ah*-compliant liquid instruments.

Notes

1. For further illustration of regulatory capital requirements for financial risks, refer to Chapter 4 of M. Crouhy, D. Galai and R. Mark (2001), *Risk Management*. New York: McGraw-Hill.
2. For further reading about the IFSB capital adequacy standards, refer to IFSB (2005b), *Capital Adequacy Standard for Institutions (other than Insurance Institutions) Offering Only Islamic Financial Services*. Kuala Lumpur: Islamic Financial Services Board.
3. Required capital is classified in the Basel Accord as Tier 1 (core capital that consists of original equity and disclosed reserves minus goodwill and investment in subsidiaries), Tier 2 (supplementary capital that consists of undisclosed reserves,

general loan loss reserves, hybrid debt instruments and asset revaluation reserves) and Tier 3 (unsecured debt). Tier 2 is limited to 50% of Tier 1 capital and Tier 3 has a maximum limit of 250% of Tier 1 capital. However, CAR has been revised and modified by Basel III.

CHAPTER 8
CONCLUSION

For Islamic banks to develop further, extend their business model and integrate with the global banking system, an integrated approach for managing risks should be implemented. A comprehensive review of risk management in Islamic banks has been developed through this book, with the presentation of an integrated risk management framework to manage the risks underlying the Islamic banking model. This framework adds to the work of the IFSB, which published guiding principles for managing the main overall risks facing Islamic financial institutions in 2005. Yet, the guidelines lack a comprehensive and integrated analysis of the underlying risks.

This book provides a comprehensive risk management framework for Islamic banks as a step towards developing the Islamic bank business model. The framework captures the main risk management process, provides an *ex post* analysis to evaluate and modify the risk management process, and ensures that regulatory aspects are in line with the banks' operations.

Islamic banks are known to have an unconventional set of risks as a result of the different financing assets on the balance sheet, each asset having a different contractual nature. Mainly because of this, adequately identifying risks for Islamic banks seems to be relatively complex. However, as explained throughout the book, risks in Islamic banks should be analysed on two levels: the overall bank level and the contractual level. On the overall level, it is clear that Islamic banks witness a similar risk map to their conventional counterparts, in which the sources of risks appear to be alike, as in the case of credit and liquidity risks. On the financial contract level, risks are analysed by examining the accounting and *Shari'ah* standards issued by the AAOIFI for each contract. After a rigorous identification of the risks, it is important to measure the risks as well as the correlation among the various risks.

To simplify the identification phase and the reporting and monitoring of risks in later steps of the risk management process, each risk should be given a code. A risk-coding system based on the classified risks for Islamic banks is presented to facilitate the analysis of the associated risks. The coding system suggests that each bank risk is provided a certain code for further reference of the risk. This was specifically designed to facilitate risk reporting and monitoring within Islamic banks. Even though many risks are similar to those of conventional banks, in some cases the severity of losses appears to be higher in Islamic banks. This results from the restrictions imposed on some operational activities, such as the prohibition of charging penalties in case of defaults, and the underdevelopment of mitigation tools. Hence, risks should be carefully measured.

Based on the similar nature of risks, widely accepted risk measurement tools from conventional banking may be used and adapted to Islamic bank risks. Similarly, some conventional mitigation strategies are also applicable to Islamic banks. Chapter 6 presents a case study elaborating on the application of an integrated risk management system to Islamic banks. A conceptual bank model was set up to demonstrate simply the process of managing risks and the application of the integrated risk management framework. A clear classification of the different deposit (investment account) facilities from a risk perspective is given, accordingly elaborating on how returns are distributed to each deposit facility. Additionally, a profit distribution model for Islamic banks is presented to elaborate on the profit distribution methods based on the risk perspective of the different deposit accounts. The presented distribution model clarifies one of the main operational differences among conventional and Islamic banks and should be useful for further risk analysis. A proper risk analysis will lead to an efficient risk management process, which is essential to maximise a firm's wealth and achieve profits. Specifically, the bank model is utilised as a case study to explain how the integrated risk management framework should be applied to Islamic banks in a way that is designed to meet the challenges of risk management currently faced by Islamic banks.

This research provides insights for regulating risks in Islamic banks, yet more research is essential in this area in order to attain internationally accepted and standardised risk regulations for Islamic banks. Islamic bank risk regulations should not only consider the specific nature of Islamic banks, but also comply with the Basel Accords, being the internationally accepted risk regulations for conventional banks. Currently, after the sub-prime crisis and with Basel III proposed at the international level, research into the compliance of Islamic banks under such regulations is much needed.

On the level of practical implications, the research provides a suitable risk management framework that could be adopted universally by Islamic banks and modified to fit different contexts. Adopting the proposed risk identification process, in practice, will not only eliminate risk definition discrepancies among Islamic banks, but also facilitate the development of a comprehensive data warehouse for all Islamic bank risks. Developing a database for Islamic bank risks would lead onto developing the use of advanced measurement models within the industry.

Due to the current status and relative newness of the Islamic banking industry, determining the integration among different risk factors represents a major challenge to the industry as Islamic banks lack the supporting data inputs. Such a challenge can only be met through a vigorous application of a fully integrated risk management framework that involves adequate reporting and identification of risks. Adequate reporting requires Islamic banks to unify the identification of the sources of the underlying risks, which currently is not the case. In view of this, this research has developed a risk-coding system based on the sources of each risk that is recommended for use by Islamic banks in identifying and reporting risks. Applying this coding system will, in time, produce a database with the required set of inputs to in turn facilitate risk analysis and incorporate correlation events. Common definitions of risks should be ensured and priority should be given to cooperation to provide an aggregate pool of information by recording risk events.

Hence, the application of an integrated risk management framework should be adopted by Islamic banks and recommended by regulatory authorities. Yet, such an application is not without challenges. The first challenge lies in the lack of a structured and uniform framework for Islamic banking. Producing such a framework requires following uniform reporting and disclosure standards, promoting transparency among industry players and harmonising *Shari'ah* standards. The AAOIFI standards represent a comprehensive set of disclosures and reporting requirements, which are not yet followed by Islamic banks. Applying the AAOIFI standards will allow comparability across Islamic banks operating in different countries and facilitate the role of supervisory and regulatory authorities. Transparency among industry players can be achieved once a standardised reporting system is followed. *Shari'ah* harmonisation is the final challenge to developing a structured Islamic finance framework. A centralised *Shari'ah* board that ensures the compliance of financial products to Islamic finance principles has become an inevitable demand.

It is recognised that infrastructure weaknesses within product development impede effective risk management (IFSB 2007: 50), so it is essential to build on a well-established and globally accepted legal Islamic finance framework. This represents the second challenge. Based on *maqasid al-Shari'ah* guidelines, such a framework should provide the elements that constitute a *Shari'ah*-compliant financial tool. The guidelines would facilitate product development and financial innovation. The underdevelopment of financial innovation within the Islamic finance industry is another challenge to risk management in Islamic banks, with developing *Shari'ah*-compliant instruments to mitigate risks and manage liquidity risk being among the main areas where work is needed. It is sometimes argued that 'too often, "innovation" is achieved by pushing the barriers and/or issuing *fatawa*[1] by taking them out of their context. Innovation ideally should be the result of a well documented and fundamental discussion on *Shari'ah* (Ghoul 2008). Product development is essential in the area of risk mitigation, which should, according to Sultan (2008), 'go through a very tight process of *Shari'ah* compliance review and endorsement'.

A third challenge is represented in the unavailability of skilled human resources. One of the main factors that should be considered by Islamic banks to support the implementation of an efficient risk management process is having qualified personnel. Abdullah and Abdul Rahman (2007) reveal that though Islamic bank managers possess knowledge regarding the general principles of Islamic banking, to enhance innovation further knowledge regarding more advanced products and *Shari'ah* principles is a prerequisite. Thus, it is recommended that more emphasis should be placed on training and educating employees and managers in advanced aspects of Islamic banks and risk management. Islamic banks should also invest in boosting risk management understanding and skills. The relatively small size of Islamic banks represents another challenge: the implementation of an integrated risk management framework and the use of more advanced conventional risk measurement tools require the use of advanced models and computer software, unaffordable items for a small business.

Finally, even though some may consider that Islamic banks are not currently in need of more sophisticated measurement methods or cannot afford to adopt such measures, it is highly recommended that Islamic banks should start developing the suitable databases that would facilitate developing and/or adopting appropriate risk measurement methods in the future. The amount of business conducted by Islamic banks is growing and, operating in a competitive market, they will be expected to keep pace with an adequate risk management system, which definitely includes appropriate measurement of risks. Adopting an adequate risk management framework will enable Islamic banks to extend their businesses into riskier activities, thus promoting higher profits and growth, and adequate risk management ensures that risk-taking decisions match the bank's capacity for absorbing possible losses. It should also be recognised that risk management is a dynamic area, which requires continuous research, as the global financial map alters constantly. To this end, an adequate application of the framework requires a multi-stakeholder collaboration of Islamic banks, regulators and supervisors to enhance the development of Islamic banks in theory and practice.

Further research is required in the area of risk measurement to validate the eligibility of the use of each of the proposed measurement methods for each Islamic bank risk. Needless to say, correlation and integration among the different risks need to be empirically tested. Similarly, risk mitigation and liquidity management in Islamic banks remain ripe areas for research, in which the development of appropriate financial instruments is essential and requires extensive and dedicated research activities.

Note

1. Plural of *fatwa*, which is a religious decree.

GLOSSARY OF ARABIC TERMS

Al-bai bithaman ajil	A deferred sale with instalment payments.
Al-ghunm bil ghurm	An Islamic finance principle that emphasises risk sharing. Earning profit is legitimised by accepting the risk/loss as it occurs.
Al-kharaj bel daman	A *Shari'ah* principle which means that if a principal amount is guaranteed, then profits and losses are attributable to the guarantor.
Al-rahn	An asset that secures a deferred obligation that can take the form of cash, gold or silver, shares in equities, or any form of tangible assets or commodities.
Amana	Refers to safe keeping or deposit in trust, and entails the absence of liability for loss.
Bai-muajjal	A deferred sale with a lump sum payment.
Fard	An obligatory duty that is subject to accountability.
Fatwa	A religious verdict by Muslim jurists (*fuqaha'*). Plural is *fatawa*.
Gharar	Literally means deception. Technically refers to situations where either party in a contract has information that is withheld from the other party or in which neither party has control over the subject of the contract.

Hamish jiddiyyah	A security deposit that is defined by the AAOIFI standards as the amount paid by the orderer in a *murabaha* contract to guarantee that the orderer is serious in his demand for the asset.
Haraam	An action that, based on the Islamic principles, is unlawful and subject to accountability if practiced.
Ijara	Islamic leasing.
Ijara Muntahia Bittamleek	A lease contract in which the ownership of the leased asset is transferred to the lessee either upon expiry at the end of the *ijara* contract or at different stages during the term of the contract.
Ijmaa	Refers to the consensus of Muslim scholars.
Ijtihad	The act of independent reasoning of *Shari'ah* scholars to deduct a judgment.
Istisna'a	A contract to manufacture.
Kafaly al darak	A credit risk mitigation method in which a client recommends a certain supplier based on the former's experience.
Makruh	A disliked action that is not subject to accountability.
Maslaha	The act of seeking benefit and repelling harm.
Mubah	A permissible action that the *Shari'ah* is indifferent of its practice.
Mudaraba	An investment contract in which one party (*rabb al-mal*) entrusts funds to another party (*mudarib*) for undertaking an activity.
Mudarib	The party in a *mudaraba* contract who undertakes a certain project and is completely responsible for its management.

Murabaha	A sale contract with a predetermined price that is not subject to change.
Musharaka	A contract based on partnership, whereby two or more partners contribute funds to carry out an investment.
Mustahab	A favourable action that would be rewarded if practiced.
Operating ijara	A lease contract that does not include a transfer of ownership of the leased asset.
Qiyas	The use of deduction by analogy through comparing and considering similar issues.
Qura'n	The holy book of Muslims, which lays down the fundamentals of the Islamic faith, including beliefs and all aspects of the Islamic way of life.
Rabb al-mal	The provider of capital in a *mudaraba* contract who provides funds to the *mudarib*.
Riba	Literally means increase or addition. It refers to the premium that must be paid by the borrower to the lender as a condition for the loan facility or an extension in its maturity.
Riba al-fadl	Referred to as *riba* of excess. One type of *riba* that occurs in certain commodities, where a commodity is exchanged for the same commodity but of an unequal amount.
Riba al-nasi'a	Referred to as *riba* of delay. It takes the form of a predetermined fixed return on a loan as a reward for waiting to be repaid.
Salam	Refers to a prepaid purchase.
Shari'ah	The Islamic law derived from the *Qura'n* and *Sunnah*.

Sukuk	Tradable Islamic certificates based on the ownership and exchange of an asset.
Sunnah	The practice and sayings of the Prophet Mohammed.
Takaful	A form of Islamic insurance based on the principle of mutual support.
Urboun	Down payment.
Wakala	A contract of agency with an agent based on a fee for services.
Zakah	One of the five pillars of Islam. Represents an obligation in respect of funds paid for a specified type of purpose and for specified categories.

ABBREVIATIONS

AAOIFI	Accounting and Auditing Organisation for Islamic Financial Institutions
ABS	Asset Backed Securities
ALM	Asset Liability Management
BIS	Bank for International Settlements
CAR	Capital Adequacy Ratio
CDO	Collateralised Debt Obligation
CDS	Credit Default Swaps
DCR	Displaced Commercial Risk
EAD	Exposure At Default
EL	Expected Losses
ES	Expected Shortfall
F-PSIA	Fixed Profit-Sharing Investment Accounts
FSA	Financial Services Board
IAHs	Investment Account Holders
IAS	International Accounting Standards
IDB	Islamic Development Bank
IFSB	Islamic Financial Services Board
IICS	Islamic Interbank Cheque Clearing System
IIFM	International Islamic Financial Markets
IIMM	Islamic Interbank Money Market
IIRA	International Islamic Rating Agency
IRB	Internal Rating-Based Approach
IRR	Investment Risk Reserves
IRTI	Islamic Research and Training Institute
LGD	Loss Given Default
LIBOR	London Interbank Offered Rate

LMC	Liquidity Management Center
PD	Probability of Default
PER	Profit Equalisation Reserves
PLS	Profit-Loss Sharing
PSIA	Profit-Sharing Investment Accounts
RAROC	Risk-Adjusted Return on Capital
UL	Unexpected Loss
VaR	Value at Risk

BIBLIOGRAPHY

AAOIFI. (2008a), *Accounting, Auditing, and Governance Standards for Islamic Financial Institutions*, Manama, Bahrain: Accounting and Auditing Organization for Islamic Financial Institutions.

AAOIFI. (2008b), *Shari'a Standards for Islamic Financial Institutions*, Manama, Bahrain: Accounting and Auditing Organization for Islamic Financial Institutions.

Abdel Karim, R. A. (1996), 'The impact of the Basel capital adequacy ratio regulation on the financial and marketing strategies of Islamic banks', *International Journal of Bank Marketing*, 14(7), 32–44.

Abdullah, R. and Abdul Rahman, A. (2007), 'Factors influencing knowledge of Islamic banking services: the case of Malaysian bank mergers', *Review of Islamic Economics*, 11(2), 31–54.

Abozaid, A. (2008), 'Contemporary Islamic financing modes between contracts technicalities and *Shari'ah* objectives', paper presented at the 8th Harvard University International Forum on Islamic Finance, Cambridge, MA, 18–20 April 2008.

Abozaid, A. (2010), 'Towards genuine *Shari'ah* products with lessons of the financial crisis', paper presented at a conference on Islamic Finance and Financial Crisis, Durham, UK, 14–15 July 2010.

Ahmed, H. (2006), 'Using RAROC in Islamic banks: value creation and risk management', paper presented at the Second International Conference on Islamic Banking:

Risk management, regulation and supervision, Kuala Lumpur, 7–8 February 2006.

Ahmed, H. (2009), 'Financial crisis: risks and lessons for Islamic finance', *ISRA International Journal of Islamic Finance*, 1(1), 7–32.

Ahmed, H. (2010), 'Assessing risk management systems: an application to Islamic banks', paper presented at the Third International Conference on Islamic Banking and Finance: Risk management, regulation and supervision, Jakarta, 23–4 February 2010.

Ahmed, H. and Khan, T. (2007), 'Risk management in Islamic banking', in M. K. Hassan and K. L. Lewis (eds), *Handbook of Islamic Banking*, Cheltenham: Edward Elgar Publishing.

Akkizidis, I. and Khandelwal, S. (2007), 'Risky business', *Islamic Business and Finance*, 15, 32–4.

Akkizidis, I. and Khandelwal, S. (2008), *Financial Risk Management for Islamic Banking and Finance*, Basingstoke: Palgrave Macmillan.

Al-Tamimi, H. A. and Al-Mazrooei, F. (2007), 'Banks' risk management: a comparison study of UAE national and foreign banks', *The Journal of Risk Finance*, 8(4), 394–409.

Allen, F. and Santomero, A. M. (1998), 'The theory of financial intermediation', *Journal of Banking and Finance*, 21, 1461–85.

Archer, S. and Abdel Karim, R. A. (2007), 'Measuring risk for capital adequacy: the issue of profit-sharing investment accounts', in S. Archer and R. A. Abdel Karim (eds), *Islamic Finance: the Regulatory Challenge*. Singapore: Wiley Asia.

Archer, S., and Haron, A. (2007). 'Operational risk exposures of Islamic banks', in S. Archer and R. A. Abdel Karim (eds), *Islamic Finance: the Regulatory Challenge*, Singapore: Wiley Asia.

Ariffin, N. M., Archer, S. and Abdel Karim, R. A. (2009), 'Risks in Islamic banks: evidence from empirical research', *Journal of Banking Regulation*, 10(2), 153–63.

BCBS. (2000a), *Credit Ratings and Sources of Credit Quality Information*, Basel: Bank for International Settlements.

BCBS. (2000b), *Principles for the Management of Credit Risk*, Basel: Bank for International Settlements.

BCBS. (2001), *Statement of the Shadow Financial Committee on the Basel Committee's Revised Capital Accord Proposal*, Basel: Bank for International Settlements.

BCBS. (2006a), *Core Principles for Effective Banking Supervision*, Basel: Bank for International Settlements.

BCBS. (2006b), *Sound Credit Risk Assessment and Valuation for Loans*, Basel: Bank for International Settlements.

BCBS. (2006c), *Sound Credit Risk Assessment and Valuation for Loans*, Basel: Bank for International Settlements.

BCBS. (2009), *Consultative Document: Proposed Enhancements for Basel II Framework*, Basel: Bank for International Settlements.

Beder, T. (1995), 'VaR: seductive but dangerous', *Financial Analysts Journal*, 51(5), 12–24.

Bessis, J. (2002), *Risk Management in Banking*, 2nd edn, Chichester: John Wiley & Sons.

Brown, K., Hassan, M. K. and Skully, M. (2007), 'Operational efficiency and performance', in M. K. Hassan and M. K. Lewis (eds), *Handbook of Islamic Banking*, Cheltenham: Edward Elgar Publishing, pp. 96–115.

Caruana, J. (2010), *Basel III: Towards a Safer Financial System*. Madrid: Bank for International Settlements.

Cecchetti, S. G. (2010), *Financial Reform: a Progress Report*. London: Bank for International Settlements.

Chapra, M. U. (2007), 'Challenges facing the Islamic

financial industry', in M. K. Hassan and M. K. Lewis (eds), *Handbook of Islamic Banking*, Cheltenham: Edward Elgar Publishing, pp. 325–60.

Chapra, M. U. and Khan, T. (2000), *Regulation and Supervision of Islamic Banks*, Occasional Paper no. 3, Jeddah: Islamic Research and Training Institute/Islamic Development Bank.

Chattha, J. A. and Bacha, O. I. (2010), 'Duration gap and net worth risk for Islamic and conventional banks: a comparative cross country analysis', *Review of Islamic Economics*, 13(2), 5–33.

Crouhy, M., Galai, D. and Mark, R. (2000), 'A comparative analysis of current credit risk models', *Journal of Banking and Finance*, 24, 59–117.

Crouhy, M., Galai, D. and Mark, R. (2001), *Risk Management*. New York: McGraw-Hill.

Cumming, C. and Hirtle, B. (2001), 'The challenges of risk management in diversified financial companies', *Economic Policy Review*, 7(1), 1–14.

Cunningham, A. (2004), *Regulation and Supervision: Challenges for Islamic finance in a Riba-based Global System*, (edited speech from World Bank Program of Seminars, 20–22 September 2003), Boston, MA: Moody's Investors Service.

Curcio, D. and Gianfrancesco, I. (2010), 'Bank pricing issues under Basel II: a multi-period risk-adjusted methodology', *Rivista Bancaria Minerva Bancaria*, 1.

Das, S. (2006), *Perfect Storms: Beautiful and True Lies about Risk Management*. London: FT-Prentice Hall.

DeutscheBank. (2004), *Credit risk Transfer Instruments: Their Use by German Banks and Aspects of Financial Stability*, Deutsche Bank Monthly Report, April 2004. See http://creditrisktransfer.free.fr/doc/bundes bank.200404mb_en_creditrisk.pdf.

Dimakos, X. and Aas, K. (2004), 'Integrated risk modelling', *Statistical Modelling*, 4, 265–77.

Dorfman, M. (2005), *Introduction to Risk Management and Insurance*, 8th edn, Upper Saddle River, NJ: Pearson Prentice Hall.

Dusuki, A. (2010), 'Can Bursa Malaysia's *Suq al-Sila'* resolve the controversy over *tawarruq*?', paper presented at the Conference on Islamic Finance and Financial Crisis, Durham, UK, 14–15 July 2010.

Elgari, M. A. (2003), 'Credit risk in Islamic banking and finance', *Islamic Economic Studies*, 10(2), 1–25.

Fallon, W. (1996), 'Calculating Value at Risk', paper presented at the conference on Risk Management in Banking, Wharton Financial Institutions Center, University of Pennsylvania, 13–15 October 1996.

Fatemi, A. and Fooladi, I. (2006), 'Credit risk management: a survey of practices', *Managerial Finance*, 32(3), 227–33.

Fiennes, T. (2007), 'Supervisory implications of Islamic banking: a supervisor's perspective', in S. Archer and R. A. Abdel Karim (eds), *Islamic Finance: the Regulatory Challenge*, Singapore: Wiley Asia.

Freeland, C. and Friedman, S. (2007), 'Risk and the need for capital', in S. Archer and R. A. Abdel Karim (eds), *Islamic Finance: the Regulatory Challenge*. Singapore: Wiley Asia.

Gassner, M. (2009), 'The current financial and economic crisis within the conventional markets: an overview', paper presented at the Harvard-LSE Workshop on Risk Management: Islamic Economic and Islamic Ethico-Legal Perspectives on the Current Financial Crisis, London School of Economics, 26 February 2009.

Ghoul, W. (2008a), 'Risk management and Islamic finance: never the twain shall meet?', *The Journal of Investing*, 17(3), 96–104.

Ghoul, W. (2008b), '*Shari'ah* scholars and Islamic finance:

towards a more objective and independent *Shari'ah*-compliance certification of Islamic financial products', *Review of Islamic Economics*, 12, 87–104.

Grais, W. and Kulathunga, A. (2007), 'Capital structure and risk in Islamic financial services', in S. Archer and R. A. Abdel Karim (eds), *Islamic Finance: the Regulatory Challenge*, Singapore: Wiley Asia.

Greuning, H. V. and Iqbal, Z. (2007), 'Banking and the risk environment', in S. Archer and R. A. Abdel Karim (eds), *Islamic Finance: the Regulatory Challenge*. Singapore: Wiley Asia.

Greuning, H. V. and Iqbal, Z. (2008), *Risk Analysis for Islamic Banks*, Washington, DC: The World Bank Group.

Haron, A. and Hock, J. L. (2007), 'Inherent risk: credit and market risks', in S. Archer and R. A. Abdel Karim (eds), *Islamic Finance: the Regulatory Challenge*, Singapore: Wiley Asia.

Hasan, M. and Dridi, J. (2010), 'The effects of the global crisis on Islamic and conventional banks: a comparative study', IMF Working Paper (WP/10/201).

Hassan, M. K. and Bashir, A. M. (2000), 'Determinants of Islamic banking profitability', paper presented at the Annual Meeting of the Economic Research Forum (ERF), retrieved 1 April 2009, from www.erf.org.eg/CMS/getFile.php?id=636.

Hassan, M. K. and Dicle, M. F. (2005), 'Basel II and regulatory framework for Islamic banks', *Journal of Islamic Economics Banking and Finance*, 1(1), 1–16.

Heffernan, S. (2005), *Modern Banking*. Chichester: John Wiley & Sons.

Heiko, H. and Cihak, M. (2008), 'Islamic banking and financial stability', *New Horizon*, http://www.newhorizon-islamicbanking.com/index.cfm?section=academicarticle&action=view&id=10702.

IFSB. (2005a), *Guiding Principles of Risk Management for Institutions (other than Insurance Institutions) Offering Only Islamic Financial Services*, Kuala Lumpur: Islamic Financial Services Board.

IFSB. (2005b), *Capital Adequacy Standard for Institutions (other than Insurance Institutions) Offering Only Islamic Financial Services*, Kuala Lumpur: Islamic Financial Services Board.

IFSB. (2007), *Islamic Financial Services Industry Development: Ten Year Framework and Strategies*, Islamic Financial Services Board, http://www.ifsb.org.

IFSB. (2010). *Islamic Finance and Global Financial Stability*, Islamic Financial Services Board, http://www.ifsb.org.

Iqbal, Z. and Mirakhor, A. (2007), *An Introduction to Islamic Finance: Theory and Practice*, Singapore: Wiley Asia.

Iqbal, M. and Molyneux, P. (2005), *Thirty Years of Islamic Banking: History, Performance and Prospects*, New York: Palgrave Macmillan.

Ismal, R. (2010), 'How do Islamic banks manage liquidity risk? An empirical survey on the Indonesian Islamic banking industry', *Kyoto Bulletin of Islamic Area Studies*, 3(2), 54–81.

Izhar, H. (2010), 'Identifying operational risk exposures in Islamic banking', *Kyoto Bulletin of Islamic Area Studies*, 3(2), 17–53.

Jabbari, A. (2006), 'A capital adequacy standard for institutions offering Islamic financial services', paper presented at the 2nd International Research Conference on Islamic Banking: Risk management, regulation and supervision, Kuala Lumpur, 7–8 February 2006.

James, M. and Andrew, H. (2008), 'French trader Kerviel cooperating with police', retrieved 4 November 2009, from http://web.archive.org/web/20080128055324/http://www.nationalpost.com/news/story.html?id=266900.

Kalapodas, E. and Thomson, M. (2006), 'Credit risk assessment: a challenge for financial institutions', *IMA Journal of Mathematics*, 17, 25–46.

Kamali, M. H. (2005), 'Fiqhi issues in commodity futures', in I. Munawar and K. Tariqullah (eds), *Financial Engineering and Islamic Contracts*. London: Palgrave Macmillan.

Khan, T. (2004), 'Risk management in Islamic banking: a conceptual framework', Islamic Research and Training Institute lecture, available at http://qfis.academia.edu.

Khan, T. and Ahmed, H. (2001), *Risk Management: an Analysis of Issues in Islamic Financial Industry*, Jeddah: Islamic Development Bank and Islamic Research and Training Institute.

Khan, M. and Bhatti, M. (2008), 'Islamic banking and finance: on its way to globalization', *Managerial Finance*, 34(10), 708–25.

Kolb, R. W. (1997), *Futures, Options and Swaps*. Malden, MA: Blackwell Publishers.

KPMG. (2008), *Frontiers in Finance*, KPMG Financial Services, https://www.kpmg.com/global/en/.

KPMG. (2011), *Basel III: Issues and Implications*, KPMG Financial Services, https://www.kpmg.com/global/en/.

Laldin, A. M. and Mokhtar, S. (2009), 'Risk management in Islamic finance', paper presented at the Harvard-LSE Workshop on Risk Management: Islamic economic and Islamic ethico-legal perspectives on the current financial crisis, London School of Economics, 26 February 2009.

Lifen, P. (2008), 'Basel II and its impact on property market in HKSAR', paper presented at the 14th Pacific Rim Real Estate (PRRE) Society Conference, retrieved 25 April 2010, from http://www.prres.net/.

Linsmeier, T. and Pearson, N. (2000), 'Value at Risk', *Financial Analysts Journal*, 56(2), 47–67.

Makiyan, S. (2008), 'Risk management and challenges in Islamic banks', *Journal of Islamic Economics Banking and Finance*, 4(3), 45–54.

Markowitz, H. (1991), 'Foundations of Portfolio Theory', *Journal of Finance*, 46(2), 469–77.

Marrison, C. (2002), *The Fundamentals of Risk Measurement*. New York: McGraw-Hill.

Mcllroy, D. H. (2008), 'Regulating risk: a measured response to the banking crisis', *Journal of Banking Regulation*, 9(4), 284–92.

McNeil, A., Frey, R. and Embrechts, P. (2005), *Quantitative Risk Management: Concepts, Techniques and Tools*, Princeton, NJ: Princeton University Press.

Metwally, M. M. (1997), 'Differences between the financial characteristics of interest-free banks and conventional banks', *European Business Review*, 97(2), 92–8.

Meyer, L. H. (2000), 'Why risk management is important for global financial institutions', paper presented at the Bank of Thailand Symposium: Risk Management of Financial Institutions, Bangkok, 31 August 2000.

Mohamed, K. and Kayed, R. (2007), 'Managing risk of Islamic equity investments: initiatives and strategies', paper presented at the International Conference on Islamic Capital Markets, Jakarta, 27–9 August 2007.

Moore, E. (2007), 'Measuring operational risk', in S. Archer and R. A. Abdel Karim (eds), *Islamic Finance: the Regulatory Challenge*. Singapore: Wiley Asia.

Muljawan, D., Dar, H. and Hall, M. A. (2004), 'Capital adequacy framework for Islamic banks: the need to reconcile depositors' risk aversion with managers' risk taking', *Applied Financial Economics*, 14, 429–41.

Obaidullah, M. (1998), 'Capital adequacy norms for Islamic

financial institutions', *Islamic Economics Studies*, 5(2), 37–55.

Obaidullah, M. (2002), 'Islamic risk management: towards greater ethics and efficiency', *International Journal of Islamic Financial Services*, 3(4).

Pyle, D. (1997), 'Bank risk management: theory', Haas School of Business, Research Program in Finance Working Paper RPF – 272.

Reuters. (2010), 'Islamic finance sets up liquidity management body', retrieved 21 November 2010, from http://in.reuters.com/article/idINIndia-52046520101008.

Rosly, S. A. and Zaini, M. A. (2008), 'Risk-return analysis of Islamic banks' investment deposits and shareholders', *Managerial Finance*, 34(10), 695–707.

Rosman, R. (2008), 'Risk management and performances of Islamic banks: a proposed conceptual framework', paper presented at the EABR and TLC Conferences, 2008.

Saita, F. (1999), 'Allocation of risk capital in financial institutions', *Journal of Financial Management*, 28(3), 95–111.

Salem, A. (2009), 'Risk management in construction industry', unpublished Masters Thesis. Faculty of Engineering, Cairo University.

Salem, R. and Badreldin, A. (2010), 'Resilience of Islamic banks', paper presented at the conference on Islamic Finance and Financial Crisis, Durham, UK, 14–15 July 2010.

Santomero, A. M. (1997), *Commercial Bank Risk Management: an Analysis of the Process*, Philadelphia, PA: The Wharton School, University of Pennsylvania.

Schierenbeck, H. and Lister, M. (2002), *Value Controlling [Grundlagen wertorientierter Unternehmensfuhrung]*, 2nd edn, Munchen: Oldenbourg Verlag.

Scholes, M. (2000), 'Crisis and risk management: the near crash of 1998', *The American Economic Review*, 90(2), 17–21.

Schoon, N. (2008), 'Islamic banking and Basel II: challenges ahead', *New Horizon*, http://www.newhorizon-islam-icbanking.com/index.cfm?section=features&action=vie w&id=10625.

Siddiqui, A. (2008), 'Financial contracts, risk and performance of Islamic banking', *Managerial Finance*, 34(10), 680–94.

Sole, J. (2007), 'Introducing Islamic banks into conventional banking systems', IMF Working Paper 07/175.

Sultan, S. (2008), 'Islamic banking: trend, development and challenges', in M. Bakar and E. Ali (eds), *Essential Readings in Islamic Finance*, Kuala Lumpur, Malaysia: CERT.

Sundararajan, V. (2004), 'Risk measurement, risk management, and disclosure in Islamic finance', paper presented at the Seminar on Comparative Supervision of Islamic and Conventional Finance, Beirut, 7–8 December 2004.

Sundararajan, V. (2007), 'Risk characteristics of Islamic products: implications for risk measurement and supervision', in S. Archer and R. A. Abdel Karim (eds), *Islamic Finance: the Regulatory Challenge*. Singapore: Wiley Asia.

Sundararajan, V. and Errico, L. (2002), 'Islamic financial institutions and products in the global financial system: key issues in risk management and challenges ahead', IMF Working Paper 02/192.

Valente, C. (2009), 'Islamic finance growth seen 10-20 pct in 3 yrs-study', *Reuters*,retrieved 26 October 2009, from http://www.reuters.com/articlePrint?articled=U SLF70613620091915.

Warde, I. (2000), *Islamic Finance in the Global Economy*. Edinburgh: Edinburgh University Press.

Wilson, R. (2009), 'Credit risk management in Islamic finance', monthly lecture presented at the Institute of Islamic Banking and Insurance, London, 16 March 2009.

INDEX

Figures are indicated by page numbers in bold. Tables are indicated by page numbers in italics.